Service First

A Business Owner's Guide to Customer Service Excellence

Travis Newton

Service First: A Business Owner's Guide to Service Excellence

Copyright © 2024. Travis Newton. All rights reserved.

No part of this book may be reproduced, stored in a retrieval system, or transmitted in any form or by any means, without the prior written permission of the publisher, except in the case of brief quotations embedded in critical articles or reviews.

Every effort has been made in the preparation of this book to ensure the accuracy of the information presented. However, the information contained in this book is sold without warranty, either express or implied. Neither the author nor its dealers or distributors will be held liable for any damages caused or alleged to be caused directly or indirectly by this book.

First published: October 2024
Edition: First
ISBN: 9798341334649

Thank you to all the great managers and supervisors I've had that always taught me to put "service first."

Dedicated to my wife, Jessica, and my children, Taylor & Greyson. I hope this inspires you to always put service first.

Table of Contents

Introduction 1

   Why "Service First"? 1

   The Importance of Customer Service Today 2

   What You'll Learn in This Book 3

   Why this Book Matters 4

Chapter 1: The Foundation of Great Customer Service 5

   The "Service First" Mindset 5

   Shifting from a Profit-First to a Service-First Approach 6

   Understanding Customer Needs 7

   Empathy and Active Listening 7

   Identifying Pain Points Before They Escalate 8

   Building a Customer-Centric Culture 9
      Embedding Customer Service into Your Company's DNA 9
      Empowering Employees to Prioritize Service 10
      Creating a Customer-Focused Mission Statement 11

   Dress for Success 12

   Attitude is Everything 13
      The Power of a Positive Attitude 13
      Remove "I Don't Know" From Your Vocabulary 14
      Smile in Your Voice 15
      Proactive vs. Reactive Attitude 16

   Summary 16

   Exercises 17

Chapter 2: Setting Clear Expectations with Customers 27

   Transparency and Communication 27

   Why Transparency Builds Trust 30

   Communicating Policies and Service Expectations 32
      How to Clearly Communicate Policies 32
      Make Policies Easy to Find 32
      Setting Service Expectations 34

   Managing Customer Expectations 36

Handling Unmet Expectations 36
Saying "No" Without Alienating the Customer 37

Setting Realistic Timelines *38*
How to Set Realistic Timelines: 39

Summary *41*

Exercises *41*

Chapter 3: Proactive vs. Reactive Service 47

The Difference Between Proactive and Reactive Service *47*

The Power of Proactive Service *49*
Why Proactive Service Builds Loyalty 49

Anticipating Customer Needs *50*

Training Your Team to be Proactive Problem Solvers *52*
Encouraging a Proactive Mindset 53
Empowering Employees to Take Action 53

Recognizing and Rewarding Proactivity *54*

Tools and Systems for Monitoring Customer Satisfaction *55*

Handling Customer Complaints Effectively *56*
Turning Complaints into Opportunities 56
Example of the L.A.S.T. Method in Action 58

Summary *59*

Exercises *60*

Chapter 4: Personalizing the Customer Experience 67

Knowing Your Customer Personally *67*

The Power of Personalization *68*

Gathering Customer Insights *68*

Using Data Wisely *69*

Small Touches, Big Impact *70*

Tailoring Your Service Approach *72*
Segmenting Your Customer Base 72
Providing Custom Solutions 73

Personalization in the Digital Age *74*
Leveraging Technology for Personalization 74

Balancing Automation and Human Interaction *75*

When to Use Automation 75
When to Stay Personal 76
Blending Automation with Personalization 76
Turning Personalization into Loyalty 77

Building Trust Through Personalization 77

Creating Repeat Customers 77

Summary 78

Exercises 78

Chapter 5: Building Long-Term Relationships with Customers 85

The Value of Loyalty 85
Why Loyal Customers Are More Valuable 85

Strategies for Building Customer Loyalty 86

Turning Transactions into Relationships 89

Building Trust Through Consistency 89

Creating Emotional Connections 89

Follow-Ups and Post-Service Care 90
The Importance of Checking In 90

Creating Lifelong Customers 90

Summary 91

Exercises 91

Chapter 6: Handling Customer Growth and Scaling Your Service 99

Growing Pains: Common Challenges When Scaling Customer Service 99

Maintaining Service Quality as You Grow 100

Keeping the Personal Touch as You Scale 104

Summary 105

Exercises 106

Chapter 7: Technology and Customer Service 113

The Role of Technology in Modern Customer Service 113
Why Technology Matters for Service 114
Leveraging Technology to Improve Service 114

Balancing Technology with the Human Touch 118
When to Automate and When to Stay Personal 118

    Maintaining Empathy in Digital Interactions 118

    The Future of Technology and Customer Service 119

    Summary 121

    Exercises 121

Chapter 8: Leading by Example 129

    Setting the Standard for Customer Service 129

    Why Leadership Matters 130

    Walking the Talk 130

        Encouraging a Customer-First Mindset 131

        Empowering Employees to Make Decisions 131

        Recognizing and Rewarding Great Service... 132

        Stepping In During Tough Situations 133

        When to Step In 133

        How to Lead in Crisis.. 134

        Building a Culture of Accountability 134

        Encouraging a Culture of Continuous Improvement............................ 135

    Summary 135

    Exercises 136

Chapter 9: Measuring and Improving Customer Service 143

    Why Measuring Customer Service is Important 143

        The Benefits of Measuring Service Performance.................................... 143

    The Key to Data-Driven Improvement... 144

        Key Metrics for Measuring Customer Service.. 144

    Gathering and Interpreting Customer Feedback 147

    Strategies for Continuous Improvement 149

    Summary 151

    Exercises 151

Chapter 10: Case Studies and Real-World Examples 159

    Case Study 1: Zappos – Building Loyalty Through Extraordinary Service 159

    Case Study 2: Ritz-Carlton – The Gold Standard of Customer Experience 161

    Case Study 3: Apple – The Power of Simplicity and Support 162

    Case Study 4: Southwest Airlines – Putting People First 163

Applying These Lessons to Your Own Business...164

Conclusion 165

Appendix A: Customer Service Checklists.......................................167

Appendix B: Tools and Resources for Managing Customer Relationships
....171

Appendix C: Training Exercises for Customer Service Teams....................175

Appendix D: Customer Service Scripts and Templates........................177

Appendix E: Crisis Management in Customer Service....................179

Appendix F: Building Customer Service into Your Company's Mission and Brand...181

Appendix G: The Role of Customer Service in Building Business Resilience 183

Appendix H: Customer Retention vs. Customer Acquisition.....................185

Appendix I: The Future of Customer Service 187

Appendix J: The Psychology of Great Customer Service.............................189

Introduction

As a business owner, you know firsthand that success isn't just about having the best product or the most competitive prices. It's about people—your customers. In an increasingly competitive market, providing exceptional customer service can set your business apart and create lasting loyalty. And that's where the **Service First** approach comes in.

In my years of running a business, I've learned that the customer experience is often the deciding factor in whether people will return or look elsewhere. It's not enough to offer a great product; you must also make customers feel valued, heard, and understood at every touchpoint. With the right approach, customer service can be a powerful tool for growth, and at the heart of that approach is putting **Service First**.

Why "Service First"?

The **Service First** method is something I developed over the years from my time working at many customer-centric companies such as Six Flags Entertainment Corporation (formerly Cedar Fair Entertainment Company) and Disney, not by reading books or taking courses, and applying those skills and lessons into my own blend in my business. It's about a shift in mindset, from thinking of customer service as just a department or a function of your business, to making it the very foundation of everything you do. It's about more than just reacting to problems—it's about proactively creating a service culture that prioritizes your customers' needs from the start.

In my business, I've faced challenges that tested my commitment to putting service above all else. Sometimes, delivering excellent service meant making tough decisions — whether it was losing a sale, bending a policy, or putting in extra time and effort to solve a customer's problem. But through these challenges, I saw firsthand the value of prioritizing long-term customer relationships over short-term profits. The return on investment? Unshakeable customer loyalty, repeat business, and a strong reputation that no marketing campaign could buy.

The Importance of Customer Service Today

In today's world, consumers have more options than ever. If they have a bad experience, they don't hesitate to leave a negative review, share their frustration on social media, or take their business elsewhere. As business owners, we must be prepared to meet their expectations and even exceed them. This means moving beyond the traditional reactive model of customer service and focusing on a more proactive, personalized approach — one that anticipates customer needs and delivers an experience that makes them feel appreciated.

Great customer service is no longer just about fixing problems; it's about preventing them from happening in the first place. It's about making every interaction, no matter how small, a positive one. This requires a genuine commitment from every part of your organization — from the owner down to the front-line staff. By making service a core value of your business, you'll not only enhance customer satisfaction but also empower your employees to become ambassadors for your brand.

What You'll Learn in This Book

In this book, I'm sharing everything I've learned about putting **Service First**—from building a customer-centric culture within your business, to handling complaints in a way that turns unhappy customers into loyal advocates, to scaling your service as your business grows. Whether you're a small business owner just starting out or an experienced entrepreneur looking to take your customer service to the next level, this guide will give you practical strategies to implement the **Service First** approach.

We'll cover key areas like:

- Understanding and anticipating customer needs
- Setting clear expectations and communicating effectively
- Personalizing the customer experience
- Managing growth without sacrificing service quality
- Training your team to deliver consistent, high-quality service

Throughout the book, you'll also find real-world examples from my own business experience, along with lessons learned from other companies that excel at customer service. The goal is to give you actionable insights that you can apply to your own business, regardless of industry or size.

Why this Book Matters

My hope is that by the time you finish reading this book, you'll have a clear understanding of what it means to put **Service First**, and you'll be ready to implement these principles in your own business. This isn't just a book about theory — it's about practical, actionable strategies that you can start using right away. Because in the end, great customer service isn't about being perfect; it's about consistently showing up, listening to your customers, and delivering value every time.
While I have employed these tactics in a technology business, they can be applied to any business type. Whether you are a local bakery, garbage collection, department store, event services, photographer, or even a Fortune 500.

So, let's get started on this journey to service excellence. Together, we'll transform the way you think about customer service — and more importantly, the way your customers experience your business.

Chapter 1: The Foundation of Great Customer Service

The "Service First" Mindset

When I first started my business, I thought success would come from simply offering a great product or service. But over time, I realized that while having a quality offering is essential, it's the service you wrap around that product or service that truly makes the difference. This is where the **Service First** mindset comes in.

The **Service First** approach is about more than just providing good customer service when something goes wrong. It's about integrating customer service into the very fabric of your business from the outset. This means placing customer satisfaction at the forefront of every decision, every interaction, and every part of your business.

It's not just about fixing problems; it's about creating a culture where customer needs are anticipated and met before they even arise. This proactive approach builds trust and fosters loyalty. Customers want to feel valued, and when they sense that you're putting them first—not just as a reactive measure but as an intentional strategy—they'll keep coming back. This chapter lays the foundation for how you can embed this mindset into your business and make **Service First** a core value.

Shifting from a Profit-First to a Service-First Approach

As business owners, it's easy to get caught up in numbers. Profit margins, quarterly earnings, and cost control are all critical to running a successful business, but when you prioritize profits over service, you end up chasing short-term gains at the expense of long-term success.

In a **Service First** business, profit is the byproduct of exceptional customer service, not the sole focus. When you prioritize service, profits naturally follow. Why? Because customers who feel valued are more likely to remain loyal, return for future purchases, and recommend your business to others. They become advocates, driving new business your way without you having to spend a dime on advertising.

Many business owners mistakenly believe that focusing on customer service means sacrificing profits, often associating service with additional costs. But investing in customer service isn't about handing out discounts or freebies. It's about creating a process that ensures every customer feels valued and appreciated. It's about empowering your team to take care of the customer, whether that means resolving an issue, answering a question, or simply making the purchasing process as smooth as possible. In return, customers are more likely to stay with your business, become repeat buyers, and spread the word.

While there may be some additional upfront costs when shifting to a **Service First** approach—such as investing in tools, employee training (and re-training), and ongoing educational campaigns to keep your team informed and skilled—these are investments in your business's long-term success. This type of investment pays dividends by fostering loyalty, driving repeat business, and boosting customer satisfaction.

Understanding Customer Needs

The first step in any **Service First** approach is understanding your customers. Too often, businesses fail to truly listen to what their customers want and need. They rely on assumptions or generic customer profiles rather than taking the time to understand the specific needs, preferences, and pain points of the people they serve.

Start by asking yourself: what do your customers value most? What problems are they trying to solve? What challenges do they face, and how can your business alleviate those challenges? These are fundamental questions that will help you design a customer experience that aligns with their needs.

Empathy and Active Listening

Empathy is at the heart of understanding your customers. It's about stepping into their shoes and seeing things from their perspective. When you listen actively—really listen—to what your customers are saying, you can uncover valuable insights that help you serve them better.

Active listening means not only hearing the words your customers are saying but also picking up on non-verbal cues and emotions. Are they frustrated? Confused? Excited? Understanding the emotional context behind a customer's words allows you to respond in a way that makes them feel heard and understood.

One of the most powerful ways to show empathy is to ask thoughtful questions and then listen attentively to the responses. For example, if a customer is having trouble with your product, instead of immediately offering a solution, ask them about their experience and what specific challenges they're facing. This not only helps you diagnose the issue more accurately but also shows the customer that you care about their experience.

Identifying Pain Points Before They Escalate

In any customer interaction, there's always the potential for frustration. Whether it's a confusing checkout process, long wait times, or unclear instructions, these pain points can turn an otherwise positive experience into a negative one. Your job, as a **Service First** business owner, is to identify and resolve these pain points before they escalate into larger problems.

One way to do this is to regularly gather feedback from your customers. Surveys, reviews, and even casual conversations can reveal valuable insights into what's working well and where improvements are needed. When you actively seek out feedback, you demonstrate to your customers that their opinion matters and that you're committed to improving their experience.

Another strategy is to anticipate potential pain points by putting yourself in the customer's shoes. Walk through your entire customer journey—from the moment they discover your business to the point where they make a purchase or use your service. Where are the friction points? Are there any moments where the process is unclear or cumbersome? By identifying these issues early, you can address them before they become a source of frustration for your customers.

Building a Customer-Centric Culture

At the core of the **Service First** method is a customer-centric culture. This isn't just about training your front-line employees to smile and be polite; it's about creating an entire business environment where customer satisfaction is the top priority.

Embedding Customer Service into Your Company's DNA

The key to creating a customer-centric culture is to make customer service an integral part of your company's identity. This means every employee, from the CEO to the entry-level team members, understands that the customer is the focal point of everything you do.

It starts with leadership. As a business owner, your commitment to customer service sets the tone for the rest of the organization. When you model the behavior and attitudes you expect from your employees, they'll follow suit. If you prioritize service, they will too. This commitment must be visible in everything you do, from how you interact with customers to the policies you put in place.

Empowering Employees to Prioritize Service

One of the most important aspects of creating a customer-centric culture is empowering your employees to make decisions that benefit the customer. Too often, employees are held back by rigid rules or the fear of making mistakes. In a Service First business, employees need the freedom to go above and beyond for customers.

This might involve allowing employees to offer solutions on the spot without waiting for managerial approval. It could also mean giving them the flexibility to handle customer complaints in a way that feels authentic and genuine. When employees are empowered to prioritize the customer's needs, they're more likely to create positive, memorable experiences.

However, this doesn't mean giving employees free rein to spend company money without limits. There needs to be a balance—employees should have enough autonomy to make a meaningful impact but operate within a realistic budget. Offering something trivial, like a free pencil or a sticker, can make customers feel belittled rather than valued. Small, insubstantial gestures can often have the opposite effect of what's intended.

For instance, in my business, I've pre-authorized employees to spend up to $100 if necessary to resolve an issue. Does this mean they hand out $100 to every customer? Of course not. But having that preauthorization allows them to act quickly and fairly when a situation calls for it. Here's an example: in the web hosting and infrastructure-as-a-service industry, we often sell out of particular server configurations. Sometimes we have another configuration in stock, but it's slightly more expensive, and the customer may have a hard budget. In cases like this, my employees can reduce the price to fit the customer's budget. We still make a profit, and the customer walks away feeling valued.

Another example comes from my experience in the amusement and theme park industry. Imagine a guest's shirt gets stained by oil from a ride warming up—a frustrating experience, to say the least. To turn the situation around, I could take the guest to a nearby gift shop, explain the situation, and allow them to choose a replacement shirt, free of charge. The same approach was used when guests had their clothing soiled by getting sick on a ride.

These gestures—whether it's offering a discount to bring a product into a customer's budget or providing a complimentary replacement for damaged clothing—can turn a negative experience into a positive one. While they may seem like small actions, they carry significant weight in the customer's perception of your business.

Creating a Customer-Focused Mission Statement

Your company's mission statement should reflect your commitment to putting customers first. A strong mission statement serves as a guiding principle for every decision you make as a business. It reminds your employees—and your customers—what you stand for and what they can expect from you.

When crafting your mission statement, think about what sets your business apart from the competition. How do you want customers to feel after interacting with your business? What promises can you make to them that align with your **Service First** values? A mission statement that emphasizes customer service not only builds trust with your customers but also inspires your team to deliver their best every day.

Dress for Success

Another important aspect of the **Service First** approach is taking pride in how your employees present themselves at work. While it may seem obvious, customers often form opinions about your business based on the appearance of your team. Although it may seem superficial, this is a bias we all have on some level. Employees who wear clean, well-fitting, and well-maintained uniforms or follow a clear dress code can help portray your business in a more professional light. On the other hand, if uniforms are inconsistent—different styles, faded colors, or in poor condition—customers may perceive your business as less professional or less cohesive.

If your business doesn't have uniforms, it's still important to encourage employees to follow a dress code that reflects the level of professionalism you want to project.

Dress codes and uniforms can elevate your business by creating a sense of professionalism and unity. You might think that as a technology business owner, I wouldn't have uniforms or a dress code, especially since much of our work is done remotely. While it's true that most of my team works from home, we still maintain a uniform policy. I had high-quality polo shirts made with our embroidered logo, and I ask my team to wear them along with nice jeans or khaki pants or shorts. You may wonder, why shorts? Well, we often work in data centers, and if you're unfamiliar with hot aisles, they're sections in data centers where servers and network equipment exhaust hot air, often reaching 100°F or more. In those conditions, comfort is important.

We wear these uniforms not just in data centers but also when interacting with customers via video calls. Even though we rarely meet customers face-to-face, the uniform helps foster a sense of teamwork and professionalism among my employees. More importantly, it affects how our business partners perceive us. When we show up looking polished and professional, it sends a message that we take our work seriously and will treat them with the same level of professionalism. In return, we're treated with the respect and courtesy that helps foster strong business relationships.

Chapter 1: The Foundation of Great Customer Service

Attitude is Everything

In a **Service First** business, attitude is foundational to the entire customer experience. The way you and your employees approach each interaction—both with customers and with each other—sets the tone for your business. It goes beyond simply smiling and speaking politely; it's about embodying a genuine willingness to help and creating an environment that values positive, solution-oriented engagement at every level.

The Power of a Positive Attitude

A positive attitude can be the difference between a frustrated customer walking away forever and a customer who feels heard, respected, and eager to return. It's not just about what you say, but how you say it. Customers can sense indifference, frustration, or confusion just as easily as they can sense care, competence, and professionalism.

Take a moment to reflect on the worst customer service experiences you've had. Think about how those situations made you feel as a customer. I can recall a recent experience at a state fair, where parking and security were managed by a third party. Employees were visibly confused and unorganized, there was no clear communication, and worst of all, they were rude to people who simply had their trunks open while parked trying to get their families ready for a fun day. It felt like chaos. There was no sense of order or professionalism, and it was obvious the employees didn't know what they were doing or how to help.

Chapter 1: The Foundation of Great Customer Service

Contrast that with a place like Disney World, where employees (with fewer numbers!) manage complex parking and security operations efficiently—and with a smile. The difference? Attitude. A **Service First** attitude creates the impression that you have everything under control, even when things are hectic.

Remove "I Don't Know" From Your Vocabulary

The phrase "I don't know" is a major stumbling block in customer service. It signals to customers that they're not going to get the help they need. It shows a lack of accountability and can quickly create frustration.

In a **Service First** business, you should remove "I don't know" from your vocabulary, and encourage your employees to do the same. Instead, replace it with, "I'm not sure, but let me find out for you." This simple shift does two things: first, it shows the customer that their question or issue matters to you, and second, it keeps the conversation moving forward toward a solution.

It's perfectly fine to not know everything—no one expects you to have all the answers on the spot. What matters is that you show a willingness to find the right answer. It's critical, however, that once you make this promise, you follow through. Whether it means reaching out to a colleague, sending an email, or making a phone call, it's essential to follow up with the customer once you have the information they need. Nothing kills customer trust faster than saying you'll find out and then failing to follow through.

Smile in Your Voice

A positive attitude isn't just something customers can see; it's something they can hear as well. Even if you're not physically smiling in every interaction, your voice should carry warmth, enthusiasm, and care. Whether you're on a phone call, a video conference, or even speaking to someone in person, the tone of your voice sends a clear message about your attitude.

When you speak with confidence and kindness, it reassures the customer that you care about their experience. On the flip side, a flat or frustrated tone can give customers the impression that you're disinterested or unhelpful, even if the words you're using are polite. This is especially important in industries where much of the communication happens over the phone or in remote environments, like my own business. Conveying professionalism and positivity through tone alone can make all the difference in how customers perceive your service.

Proactive vs. Reactive Attitude

The service experience at the state fair demonstrated a reactive, confused approach to customer service. Employees were clearly unsure of what to do and had no cohesive plan for managing the situation. The result? Confusion and frustration for everyone involved. When employees are reactive—waiting for problems to escalate before they step in—customers are already frustrated by the time help arrives.

In contrast, a **Service First** attitude is proactive. It's about anticipating customer needs and resolving issues before they become problems. In a well-run business, employees don't wait for someone to complain — they look for opportunities to assist customers and make their experience better. A proactive attitude creates confidence and calm in high-pressure situations, making your business stand out in the customer's mind.

Summary

By embracing a **Service First** mindset, you're laying the foundation for a business that thrives on customer satisfaction and loyalty. This chapter has outlined how shifting your focus from profit to service can ultimately drive long-term success, while also highlighting the importance of building a culture that empowers employees to prioritize customer needs.

Key elements of the **Service First** approach include:

- **Attitude is Everything**: A positive, solution-oriented attitude is essential not only when interacting with customers but also internally among team members. By encouraging your employees to approach challenges with optimism and professionalism, you create an environment where customers feel valued and respected.

- **Remove "I Don't Know"**: Eliminate the phrase "I don't know" from your vocabulary and replace it with "I'm not sure, but I'll find out." This subtle shift in language keeps the conversation moving forward and demonstrates your commitment to helping the customer.

- **Dress for Success**: Appearance matters. Whether it's a uniform or a simple dress code, how your employees present themselves reflects the professionalism of your business. When employees look the part, customers are more likely to perceive your business as organized, competent, and reliable.

- **Proactive Service**: Rather than waiting for issues to arise, train your team to anticipate customer needs and address potential problems before they escalate. This proactive approach ensures smoother experiences and leaves a lasting positive impression.

As you move forward, remember: putting service first isn't just good for your customers — it's good for your business. By prioritizing a customer-centric culture and adopting these principles, you'll position your business to stand out in today's competitive market, driving loyalty, advocacy, and long-term growth.

Exercises

Exercise 1: Shifting from Profit-First to Service-First

In this exercise, you'll reflect on how your business currently balances profit and service and identify ways to prioritize customer experience without sacrificing long-term success.

Steps:

1. **List 3 ways** your business currently focuses on maximizing profits (e.g., upselling products, reducing operational costs, or minimizing customer service response times to save resources).

2. **Now, list 3 ways** you could shift to a **Service First** approach that focuses on customer experience without sacrificing long-term profitability (e.g., empowering

employees to resolve customer issues without approval, offering personalized service, or improving response times for customer inquiries).

3. **Reflection**: How do you think shifting these practices would impact customer loyalty and business growth over time? Write a short paragraph on how these changes could influence your long-term success.

Exercise 2: Understanding Your Customer

To provide excellent service, you first need to deeply understand your customer's needs, pain points, and expectations.

Steps:

1. **Create a profile** for your ideal customer. Consider their demographics, needs, challenges, and how your product or service helps them.

2. **Answer the following questions**:
    - What does my customer value most in their interactions with my business?
    - What are the common frustrations or challenges my customers face?
    - What steps can I take to make their experience smoother and more satisfying?

3. **Action Plan**: Based on your answers, list two practical ways you can improve the customer experience based on these insights.

Exercise 3: Empowering Your Employees

Empowering employees is key to creating a service-first culture. This exercise will help you think about how your team can be more empowered to provide exceptional service.

Steps:

1. **Review your current policies**: Identify one or two areas where employees have limited decision-making power (e.g., needing manager approval for refunds, discounts, or resolving customer complaints).

2. **List 2 ways** you can empower your employees to resolve customer issues more effectively (e.g., allowing them to offer on-the-spot solutions, increasing the budget they can use for resolving customer issues without approval).

3. **Reflection**: Write down one challenge you think your employees might face if given more authority, and outline how you'll support them in overcoming this challenge (e.g., training, regular check-ins, or setting clear guidelines for empowered decision-making).

Exercise 4: Anticipating Customer Needs

Anticipating customer needs can help you provide proactive service and prevent issues before they arise.

Steps:

1. Think of **two common problems** your customers experience when interacting with your business (e.g., confusion about product features, difficulty reaching customer support, or long delivery times).

2. **Brainstorm ways** you could proactively address these issues before they happen (e.g., sending a how-to guide or FAQ after purchase, reducing wait times with automated responses).

   3. **Implementation**: Choose one idea from your list and develop a plan for how you'll implement this proactive service strategy over the next month.

Exercise 5: Creating a Customer-Centric Culture

Building a **Service First** business requires cultivating a customer-centric culture within your team. Use this exercise to reflect on your company's current culture and identify opportunities for improvement.

Steps:

   1. **Evaluate your current culture**: On a scale of 1-10, rate how customer-centric your business culture is. Do you and your team regularly prioritize customer satisfaction over immediate profits?

   2. **Brainstorm** three ways you could strengthen your company's customer-first culture (e.g., incorporating customer feedback into decision-making, offering regular customer service training for your team, or recognizing employees who go above and beyond for customers).

   3. **Action Plan**: Pick one of the three ideas you brainstormed and outline specific steps you'll take to implement this cultural shift in your business over the next quarter.

Exercise 6: Service-First Customer Journey Mapping

In this exercise, you'll map out a typical customer's journey with your business and identify key moments where you can enhance their experience.

Steps:

1. **List the key stages** in your customer journey—from discovery to post-purchase support (e.g., researching your products, placing an order, receiving their purchase, contacting support).

2. **Identify 3-5 touchpoints** where your business could improve the customer experience (e.g., better website navigation, faster shipping, proactive customer follow-up).

3. **Improvement Plan**: Choose one touchpoint and write a plan for how you'll enhance the customer experience at that stage (e.g., updating your website for better usability, improving communication after a purchase).

Exercise 7: Attitude is Everything

Attitude is the core of customer service. This exercise will help you assess your team's attitude and identify areas for improvement.

Steps:

1. **Reflect on a recent customer interaction**: Was the attitude of the employee involved positive, solution-oriented, and customer-focused? How did the customer react to the tone of the interaction?

2. **Identify 2 behaviors** that you want your employees to exhibit in every customer interaction (e.g., offering help before being asked, using positive language).

3. **Action Plan**: Develop a plan for how you will reinforce these behaviors with your team. This could include training sessions, regular feedback, or rewards for employees who consistently demonstrate the right attitude.

Exercise 8: Removing "I Don't Know"

This exercise helps you train your team to avoid saying "I don't know" and encourages a more helpful, solution-oriented approach.

Steps:

1. **Reflect on past situations**: Think of a time when you or one of your employees said "I don't know" to a customer. How did the customer react? How could the situation have been handled differently?

2. **Practice**: Write down alternative phrases that employees can use instead of "I don't know," such as "I'm not sure, but let me find out for you" or "I'll look into that and get back to you shortly."

3. **Role-Play**: Have your employees practice using these alternative phrases in various customer service scenarios. This can help them get comfortable with providing a solution-oriented response even when they don't have the answer immediately.

Exercise 9: Smile in Your Voice

Chapter 1: The Foundation of Great Customer Service

The tone of your voice matters as much as the words you say. This exercise will help you and your team practice conveying warmth and professionalism, even when the customer can't see your face.

Steps:

1. **Evaluate your team's communication**: Choose a recent phone call or video chat with a customer. Did the employee sound engaged, friendly, and professional? How did the customer respond?

2. **Practice smiling while speaking**: Have your team practice speaking on the phone or in a video call while consciously smiling. Discuss how this changes the tone of their voice and how they think it affects the customer's perception.

3. **Reflection**: Encourage employees to reflect on how using a warm, friendly tone can make a positive difference in customer interactions, and how tone of voice affects customer emotions and trust.

Exercise 10: Dressing for Success

Appearance matters, even in a remote work environment or industries where face-to-face contact is limited. This exercise will help you think about how your team's appearance affects your business's image.

Steps:

1. **Evaluate your team's current dress code**: Whether it's casual or formal, how does it align with the professionalism you want to project to customers and

partners? Does it convey consistency and pride in the work being done?

2. **List 2 adjustments** you can make to your team's appearance or dress code to align more closely with your brand (e.g., providing branded uniforms or shirts, setting a clear dress code for video calls or in-person meetings).

3. **Reflection**: Write a short paragraph on how dressing professionally and consistently could impact the perception of your business and the respect it earns from customers and partners.

Exercise 11: Proactive vs. Reactive Service

A **Service First** business is proactive, not reactive. This exercise will help you and your team think about how to anticipate customer needs before problems arise.

Steps:

1. **List 3 common issues** your customers face when interacting with your business (e.g., long wait times, confusion about product features, billing issues).

2. **Brainstorm proactive solutions**: Identify how you could address these issues before they escalate (e.g., sending out product tips, improving communication about delivery times, or adding FAQs on your website).

3. **Action Plan**: Choose one of these proactive solutions and create a timeline for implementing it in your business over the next month.

Chapter 1: The Foundation of Great Customer Service

Chapter 2: Setting Clear Expectations with Customers

One of the biggest contributors to customer dissatisfaction is the mismatch between what customers expect and what a business delivers. In a **Service First** business, setting clear expectations is essential to building trust, maintaining transparency, and creating an overall positive customer experience. When customers know exactly what to expect from your business — from pricing to policies to service timelines — they feel more confident in their interactions with you. They can make informed decisions and are less likely to be frustrated or surprised when things don't go exactly as planned.

In this chapter, we'll explore how setting clear expectations early on helps avoid misunderstandings, prevent disputes, and foster a more trusting relationship with your customers. You'll learn practical techniques for communicating openly and transparently, and how to manage expectations when things go wrong.

Transparency and Communication

At the heart of setting clear expectations is communication. Transparency is not just about being honest when something goes wrong; it's about being upfront and clear with your customers from the very beginning. In a world where customers are often bombarded with confusing or misleading information, offering clarity can be a breath of fresh air.

Don't confuse "transparency" with "oversharing." There is a big distinction between the two. For example, posting everyone's lunch and break schedules could be seen as oversharing or unnecessary information, but a simple message like, "Our Customer Service team takes lunch between 12 PM and 1 PM, so response times may be slower during that hour," is a good example of transparency. It provides customers with useful information without overwhelming them with details they don't need.

Likewise, you don't have to say that your business is understaffed. A more transparent yet professional way to explain this could be: "We're currently experiencing a higher-than-usual volume of inquiries, so our response times may be slightly delayed. We appreciate your patience and are working hard to get back to everyone as quickly as possible." This type of transparency sets realistic expectations for the customer, keeps them informed, and maintains trust without revealing internal struggles that might undermine confidence in your business.

When possible, it's even more helpful to offer specific details. For example, you could explain: "If you call us, the expected hold time is around 20 minutes, but if you send us an email, we should be able to respond within 5 minutes." Providing customers with concrete expectations allows them to make informed decisions about how they engage with your business. It also shows that you respect their time and are actively working to make their experience as seamless as possible.

Chapter 2: Setting Clear Expectations with Customers

Being specific removes ambiguity, which is crucial in a **Service First** business. Customers appreciate clarity, and when you're upfront about wait times or other service factors, it helps them feel in control of their experience. As I'll discuss further in the chapter on technology and service, your goal should be to remove as much vagueness as possible. The clearer you can be, the less room there is for misunderstandings or frustration.

It's also important to remember that transparency doesn't just mean giving customers information — it means setting expectations that you strive to exceed. For instance, if you tell a customer to expect a 5-minute wait but they're helped in 2 minutes, they'll be pleasantly surprised and more likely to leave with a positive impression. But be careful: there's a fine line between setting realistic expectations and intentionally inflating wait times to create the illusion of "under-promising and over-delivering." This tactic may work once or twice, but over time, customers will notice, and it can backfire by creating distrust.

Honesty is the cornerstone of transparency. Customers value accuracy and consistency. If you're honest about what to expect, even if it's not what they want to hear, they will appreciate your straightforwardness. Conversely, if they feel you've manipulated their expectations for the sake of exceeding them, it undermines the trust you're trying to build. The key is to offer accurate estimates, aim to exceed them naturally, and focus on providing consistent, high-quality service.

By being transparent, specific, and honest in your communication, you set a strong foundation for building trust with your customers. They'll know they can rely on your business to keep them informed and handle their needs professionally — whether things are running smoothly or you're facing challenges behind the scenes.

The goal of transparency is to create clarity and build trust. Customers don't expect perfection, but they do expect honesty and straightforward communication. When they feel informed and in the loop, they are more likely to trust your brand — even when things aren't going perfectly.

By setting clear expectations through transparent communication, you show customers that you respect their time and value their relationship. This, in turn, strengthens customer loyalty and fosters a deeper connection between them and your business.

Why Transparency Builds Trust

When customers know exactly what they're getting, they are more likely to feel confident in their decision to do business with you. By being transparent, you show your customers that you respect their time, money, and intelligence. This fosters a stronger relationship, one built on mutual respect.

Being transparent means communicating honestly about all aspects of your business:

- **Pricing**: Be upfront about costs, including any additional fees that may apply. Hidden fees are one of the quickest ways to lose customer trust.

- **Timelines**: Whether it's how long a service will take or when a product will be delivered, managing time expectations is critical to customer satisfaction.

- **Processes**: Clearly explain how your services work, the steps involved, and what customers can expect along the way.

Think about a time when you were quoted a price but ended up having to pay more. How did that make you feel? For example, in the web hosting industry, it's common for providers to advertise, "Buy web hosting today for $2.00 per month," only for customers to discover during checkout that it requires a multi-year contract, additional services, and results in a final charge of $350. This bait-and-switch tactic breeds frustration and breaks trust.

Another example: imagine going to make a purchase and pulling out your credit card, only to be told that there's a "convenience fee" added at the last minute. Why wasn't this disclosed upfront? It's a small fee, but it still leaves a bad taste. The business could have built the fee into the cost or, at the very least, disclosed it earlier. Surprise fees, no matter how small, can leave customers feeling blindsided and deceived.

It's important to note that transparency doesn't mean overwhelming your customers with every tiny detail. It's about sharing the right information at the right time, in a way that's easy for them to understand. The more transparent you are, the fewer surprises customers will encounter, which leads to greater satisfaction.

Communicating Policies and Service Expectations

Every business has policies, whether it's regarding returns, warranties, or customer service response times. One of the most common mistakes businesses make is assuming that customers will read or understand these policies without clear communication. In a **Service First** business, it's your responsibility to ensure that your customers are fully informed and aware of how your business operates.

How to Clearly Communicate Policies

Make Policies Easy to Find

Don't hide your terms and conditions, return policy, or other important information in the fine print. Display key policies prominently on your website, within emails, or during the purchasing process. This ensures that customers see them at relevant points in their journey. While it might be tempting to make the "Terms and Conditions" link blend into the background of your website, resist the urge. It should be a normal link, presented clearly alongside other navigation links.

Simplify the Language

Avoid using overly complex or legalistic language. Break down your policies in a way that's easy for customers to understand. For example, instead of saying, "The customer shall return the product in an unused and undamaged state within 30 days of the purchase date," say, "You can return any unused item within 30 days for a full refund." Of course, where legal language is required, make sure it's there. Something I like to do is create two versions of policies: one that's written in plain, human-readable language, and one that's more formal for legal purposes. Both versions should link to each other, allowing customers to choose which they'd like to read.

Proactively Communicate Critical Policies

If there's a policy that could significantly impact a customer's experience—such as a no-return policy on certain items—proactively communicate this before they make a purchase. It's far better to lose a sale upfront than to deal with a frustrated or upset customer later. Don't try to hide these policies in small print or fine details. Present them in the same font size as the rest of the text on the page, ensuring customers are fully informed before making a decision.

Setting Service Expectations

Customers need to know what to expect when it comes to the service they'll receive. This could involve how long it takes for their order to be fulfilled, how soon they'll hear back from customer service, or what steps to take if they encounter a problem. Setting these expectations from the start can prevent unnecessary frustration later on and create a smoother experience for everyone.

In the web hosting industry, we use the term "Service Level Agreement" (SLA). This is a formal agreement we make with customers outlining important details like hardware replacement timeframes, server availability (uptime), and how long it takes to respond to support tickets. Essentially, it sets clear expectations for the level of service the customer will receive.

Here are some key factors to consider when setting service expectations:

- **Timeframes**: Whether it's shipping, support response times, or project deadlines, be upfront about how long customers should expect to wait. Collect data over time to evaluate whether the timeframes you've set are too strict or too loose and adjust them accordingly.

- **Availability**: Let customers know when and how they can reach you, whether it's during business hours or through various channels like email, phone, or live chat. Set goals for both response times and resolution times. However, be cautious with resolution times—don't mark an issue as resolved until the customer confirms that it is.

- **Responsiveness**: When customers reach out with questions or concerns, provide them with a clear timeframe for when they can expect a response. Even an automated email acknowledging their request — such as, "We've received your message and will get back to you within 24 hours" — can ease anxiety and reassure them that their inquiry is being handled.

By setting these expectations early on, customers won't be left wondering what to do or when they'll hear back from you. This reduces their anxiety and improves their overall experience, making them more likely to trust and return to your business.

Consider the following scenario: I needed to get some work done on my car and wanted to shop around for the best price. I reached out to several auto repair shops, many of which had contact forms on their websites. To my surprise, only one shop actually got back to me, and I'm still waiting to hear from the others! Because those other shops never responded, I assumed they were too busy to handle new business.

The one shop that did respond got back to me within an hour. They answered all of my questions, gave me an exact price — including taxes and fees — so there were no hidden surprises. They even told me what time I could expect to be out of the shop if I came in at a certain time. So, I chose that shop, and sure enough, I paid exactly what they quoted and was out by the time they promised. Needless to say, I'll be going back to that shop.

Managing Customer Expectations

While transparency and proactive communication can prevent many issues, there will inevitably be times when customer expectations don't align with what your business can realistically deliver. In a **Service First** business, managing these situations with honesty and tact is crucial.

Handling Unmet Expectations

When you can't meet a customer's expectations, the way you handle the situation can make all the difference. If a customer expects something you can't provide, it's important to address the issue head-on rather than avoiding it. Here's how:

1. **Acknowledge the Gap**: Start by acknowledging that there's a gap between what the customer expected and what you're able to deliver. This validates their concerns and shows empathy.

2. **Provide a Clear Explanation**: Without getting defensive, explain why the expectation can't be met. Be honest but tactful. For example, if a customer is upset about a delay, explain the reason for the delay and what you're doing to address it.

3. **Offer Alternatives**: Whenever possible, provide an alternative solution. If you can't meet their original request, offer something that still adds value — whether it's a discount, a refund, or a different product or service.

Saying "No" Without Alienating the Customer

There are times when you'll need to say no to a customer's request, either because it's unreasonable or outside your business's capabilities. In a **Service First** business, how you say no is just as important as why you say it. A well-communicated "no" can still leave a customer feeling respected and valued.

Here are some ways to say no while maintaining a positive relationship:

- **Be Clear and Direct**: Avoid ambiguity. Customers appreciate a straightforward answer more than a vague one that leaves them unsure of what to expect. It's better to say, "This is outside the scope of our knowledge and skills right now," than to offer a generic, "We're unable to do this." Clear communication sets proper expectations and shows that you respect the customer enough to be honest.

- **Show Empathy**: Let the customer know that you understand their request and why it's important to them. Showing that you care about their needs makes the rejection feel less harsh. You might say, "I wish we could help you with this, as I understand it would make things much easier for you," to soften the impact of the "no" and show that their situation matters to you.

- **Offer a Solution**: If you can't meet their request, suggest an alternative that might address their issue or solve their problem. For example, if a customer requests a product that's out of stock, offer to notify them when it becomes available, or suggest a similar item. If they're asking for a service that you can't provide, you could recommend another business that can fulfill the request. Offering alternatives keeps the door open for future interactions and shows your commitment to helping the customer, even if indirectly.

Saying "no" doesn't have to be a negative experience, and often customers are more than reasonable when given a clear and respectful answer. It's all about how you communicate the rejection—when done right, you can maintain a positive relationship and keep customers coming back.

Setting Realistic Timelines

One of the most common sources of frustration for customers is unmet deadlines. Whether it's waiting for a product to be delivered or a service to be completed, customers rely on the timelines you provide. If those timelines aren't realistic, you risk disappointing your customers.

How to Set Realistic Timelines:

Be Conservative

Always give yourself a buffer when estimating timelines. If you think a service will take three days, tell the customer it will take five. This way, if something goes wrong, you'll have room to address the issue without breaking your promise. I like to follow a simple rule when planning: **"Always expect the unexpected."** There are countless factors outside of anyone's control—such as unexpected weather, utility failures, or illnesses—that can cause delays. For example, if you're a paving company and need to pave a driveway during a rainy season, you should expect potential rain delays and factor them into your schedule. If everything goes smoothly, you'll finish earlier than expected, leaving the customer impressed with your efficiency.

Communicate Changes Immediately

If there's going to be a delay, don't wait until the deadline has passed to inform your customer. Let them know as soon as you're aware of the issue and provide an updated timeline. Think of it this way: would you prefer your employees to tell you they need a day off at the start of the workday or as soon as they know they'll need the time off? The same principle applies to your customers. If something in a project needs to change, inform them immediately, not at the last minute.

Explain the Reasoning

If you anticipate that something will take longer than the customer expected, explain why. Customers are far more understanding when they know the reasoning behind a delay, especially if it's out of your control. Returning to the driveway paving example, if you need to reschedule due to a sudden rain forecast, explain to the customer: **"We need to reschedule because the forecast shows rain, and we can't pave in wet conditions, as it compromises the integrity of the asphalt."** Clear communication helps customers appreciate your professionalism and the steps you're taking to ensure quality service.

Leverage Past Data

If your business has been around for a while, you've likely gathered valuable data on how long certain jobs or services take. This data can come from employee timecards, job notes, or just general experience. Tap into this knowledge to calculate median job completion times and set more accurate expectations.

For example, in my business, we deploy servers regularly. If I order hardware from a particular vendor, I know that it generally takes around two weeks for the equipment to arrive at the data center. So, when quoting customers, I tell them to expect about 2.5 weeks, providing an extra buffer of a few days to account for the unexpected. On the other hand, I can sometimes deploy a server in just five hours, but I'll still quote 12 hours to allow for potential issues like operating system installation hiccups, finding space for the server, or making hardware adjustments to meet the customer's specifications.

By building in these buffers, you can exceed expectations when things go smoothly, and you'll have enough time to resolve any unexpected challenges without disappointing the customer.

Summary

Setting clear expectations with your customers is a critical aspect of delivering excellent service. By being transparent and communicating proactively, you build trust and prevent misunderstandings before they occur. When expectations aren't aligned, managing them with empathy and offering alternatives can turn a potentially negative experience into a positive one. Remember, in a **Service First** business, your goal is to ensure that customers feel informed, respected, and valued at every step of their journey with you. The clearer and more transparent you are, the more likely you are to create a loyal, satisfied customer base that knows exactly what to expect from your business.

Exercises

Exercise 1: Evaluating Your Current Policies for Transparency

Take a look at the current policies you have in place for your business, whether they involve pricing, timelines, or customer service.

Steps:

1. **Select 3 policies** you currently have in place (e.g., return policy, shipping times, support response times).
2. **Ask yourself**:

- Are these policies easy for customers to find and understand?
- Is the language clear, or does it contain legal jargon that might confuse customers?

3. **Rewrite one policy** to simplify the language, making it clear and easy for your customers to understand. This should be a "human-readable" version that aligns with your business's transparency goals.

Exercise 2: Setting Realistic Expectations

Setting expectations is crucial for delivering great customer service. This exercise will help you evaluate and refine the expectations you set for your customers.

Steps:

1. **Choose a common service or process** in your business (e.g., shipping times, project completion times, or customer support response times).

2. **Review past performance data**: How often did you meet, exceed, or fall short of your estimated timeframes? If you don't have data, think about your general experience in this area.

3. **Adjust your time estimates**: Based on your findings, adjust your timeframes to better reflect reality while still leaving room for unexpected delays. Add a buffer to your estimates that allows for unforeseen issues without significantly delaying delivery or service.

4. **Reflection**: How do you think these adjusted timeframes will impact customer satisfaction?

Exercise 3: Communicating Delays

Delays are sometimes inevitable, but how you communicate them can make all the difference in preserving customer trust.

Steps:

1. **Think of a recent situation** where your business experienced a delay (e.g., a late product delivery or missed project deadline).

2. **Evaluate how the delay was communicated**: Did you notify the customer as soon as you knew about the delay, or did you wait until the deadline had already passed?

3. **Write a sample email or message** you would send to a customer in the future, explaining a delay as soon as you become aware of it. Include:

   - The reason for the delay.
   - The revised timeline.
   - Reassurance that you are still committed to delivering the best possible outcome.

Exercise 4: Practicing Empathy in Customer Interactions

Empathy can go a long way when saying no to a customer or explaining a delay. This exercise will help you and your team practice showing empathy in tough situations.

Steps:

1. **Think of a scenario** in which you need to say no to a customer or explain a delay (e.g., a product is out of stock, or a service is not available).

2. **Write two responses** to the customer's request:
    - One that simply says no or explains the delay.
    - One that includes empathy, offers a solution, and maintains a positive tone (e.g., "I understand how important this is to you, and I wish we could help, but here's what we can do instead...").
3. **Compare the two responses**: Reflect on how the second response might make the customer feel more valued and help maintain a positive relationship.

Exercise 5: Creating Transparency in Pricing

Pricing transparency is one of the most important factors in building trust with customers. This exercise will help you assess how transparent your pricing structure is and identify areas for improvement.

Steps:

1. **Review your current pricing**: Are there any hidden fees or costs that customers might not be aware of until later in the purchasing process?
2. **Ask yourself**:
    - How could I make my pricing more transparent?
    - Are there any common customer complaints or surprises related to pricing?
3. **Make one change** to improve your pricing transparency. This could involve updating your website, revising your invoice layout, or ensuring that all fees are disclosed upfront.

Exercise 6: Setting Customer-Focused SLAs (Service Level Agreements)

SLAs help set clear expectations for customers, especially in industries where service levels matter.

Steps:

1. **Choose one area of service** in your business where customers frequently have expectations about performance (e.g., response times, product delivery, or service completion).

2. **Create a basic SLA**: Identify key performance metrics you can realistically commit to (e.g., "We will respond to support tickets within 24 hours" or "Orders will be shipped within 3 business days").

3. **Add a buffer**: Include a reasonable buffer to account for unexpected delays, but don't inflate the times too much. Consider adding a clause for notifying the customer immediately if a delay arises.

4. **Reflection**: How do you think creating and communicating this SLA will affect customer satisfaction and trust?

Exercise 7: Managing Customer Expectations Proactively

Being proactive with customers helps build trust and reduces frustration. This exercise will help you think about how to be more proactive in your communication.

Steps:

1. **Identify a service or product** in your business that commonly faces delays or challenges (e.g., seasonal delays, shipping issues, or high-demand products).

2. **Think of a proactive communication strategy**: How can you inform customers about potential issues before they even ask? For example, sending an email update when demand spikes, or placing a banner on your website during high-volume periods.

3. **Create a draft message**: Write a proactive message you could send to customers, letting them know what to expect and how you plan to address any challenges.

Exercise 8: Leveraging Data to Improve Estimates

Data can help you set more realistic expectations and better manage customer satisfaction.

Steps:

1. **Look at past performance data**: Whether it's how long it takes to fulfill orders, complete projects, or respond to inquiries, gather data that reflects your actual performance.

2. **Analyze your findings**: Are there areas where your estimates have been too optimistic or too conservative?

3. **Adjust your future estimates**: Based on the data, adjust your timeframes and expectations to better match reality while still allowing for a reasonable buffer.

4. **Track the results**: After making these changes, track how closely your new estimates align with actual performance. This will help you continue refining your processes.

Chapter 3: Proactive vs. Reactive Service

In many businesses, customer service is primarily reactive. The team responds to complaints, fixes issues after they've been identified, and deals with dissatisfied customers only when things go wrong. While reactive service is necessary — there will always be issues to fix — the true power of exceptional customer service lies in being proactive.

In a **Service First** business, the goal is not to wait for problems to arise, but to prevent them from happening in the first place. Proactive service anticipates customer needs, addresses potential issues before they escalate, and creates a positive experience even when things don't go perfectly. This chapter explores the difference between reactive and proactive service, how to shift toward a more proactive approach, and how this mindset can transform your business.

The Difference Between Proactive and Reactive Service

To better understand the importance of proactive service, let's first define the difference between reactive and proactive approaches.

Chapter 3: Proactive vs. Reactive Service

Reactive Service is the traditional way of handling customer service. It occurs when customers reach out to report an issue, make a complaint, or ask for help. While reactive service is essential, it often results in a frustrated customer — someone who's already had a negative experience and is looking for a solution.

Examples of reactive service:

- A customer emails support because they received a defective product.

- A customer calls because their shipment is late.

- A customer leaves a negative review after a poor experience, prompting the business to reach out.

While these situations need to be addressed, they represent a missed opportunity for a more proactive approach.

Proactive Service, on the other hand, is about anticipating customer needs and resolving issues before they arise. It involves staying ahead of potential problems, providing valuable information before customers ask for it, and creating a seamless experience that reduces the likelihood of frustration.

Examples of proactive service:

- Notifying customers about potential shipping delays before they reach out.

- Offering tips or tutorials on how to use a product after it's purchased.

- Regularly checking in with customers after their purchase to ensure they're satisfied.

Proactive service is a hallmark of a **Service First** business because it demonstrates that you care about your customers' experience—not just when things go wrong, but every step of the way.

The Power of Proactive Service

Why Proactive Service Builds Loyalty

When customers feel like you're taking care of their needs before they even have to ask, it builds trust and loyalty. They appreciate that you've gone out of your way to make their experience better without them needing to do anything. This creates a sense of goodwill, making customers more likely to return, recommend your business, and feel positive about their interactions with you.

For example, imagine a customer orders a product, and the shipping company you use is experiencing delays. If you reach out proactively to inform the customer of the delay, apologize for the inconvenience, and provide an updated delivery estimate, the customer feels informed and valued. In contrast, if the customer has to chase you down for an explanation after their package arrives late, they're left feeling frustrated and disappointed.

Proactive service turns potential negative experiences into positive ones. It shows your customers that you're on their side and that you're working to make things right before they even realize there's an issue.

Another example comes from my firsthand experience as a web hosting provider. We monitor the activity in our data center, and if we notice that a customer's server isn't as active as it usually is, we reach out if the change seems significant. Perhaps the customer accidentally shut down their server and didn't realize it. Maybe they're experiencing an issue with their server and are unaware of it. A simple proactive check-in can impress a customer and even win additional business. These small actions show that you're not just reactive but are actively looking out for your customers' best interests.

Anticipating Customer Needs

To deliver proactive service, you need to understand your customers' needs and anticipate potential problems before they occur. This requires gathering feedback, recognizing patterns, and thinking ahead.

Here are some ways to anticipate customer needs:

Listen to Feedback

Pay attention to the feedback customers give you—both positive and negative. If you notice a pattern of customers having difficulty with a particular product feature or process, address it proactively. For example, if multiple customers are confused about your return process, create a simple guide or FAQ that explains it clearly and make it easy to find. If customers struggle to understand how a feature or product works, try to identify the root of the issue. In software applications, you can use tools like "hot spot" tracking to record user sessions and see where customers are getting hung up. If it's a physical product, invite customers to show you how they're using it, which can reveal areas where you can improve the design or instructions.

Look for Patterns

Are there certain times of the year when you receive more complaints about a particular service? Do customers frequently ask the same question after making a purchase? Identifying patterns allows you to anticipate common issues and address them before they become widespread. Early in my career, I worked for a company that had purchased a large batch of new laptops for employees. After a few weeks, I began receiving reports of failing hard drives. I quickly noticed a pattern: the drives were failing roughly two weeks after deployment. Anticipating further failures, I proactively ordered new hard drives so I could replace them faster, minimizing downtime and getting employees back to work quickly.

Chapter 3: Proactive vs. Reactive Service

Use Technology

Leverage tools like customer relationship management (CRM) systems, data analytics, and automated messaging to stay one step ahead of customer needs. For example, you can send automated emails to new customers with helpful information about their recent purchase, or use predictive analytics to identify which customers might need follow-up support. These tools can help you track customer behavior, allowing you to offer solutions before issues arise.

Offer Help Before It's Requested

If you know that customers often struggle with a specific part of your process, don't wait for them to reach out for help. For instance, if you sell software, send an email with installation tips or common troubleshooting advice as soon as the customer makes a purchase. By proactively offering help, you save your customers the frustration of having to search for solutions themselves, and you show that you care about their experience from the start.

Training Your Team to be Proactive Problem Solvers

A proactive service approach requires a shift in how your entire team thinks about customer service. Instead of waiting for problems to come to them, your employees should be actively looking for ways to improve the customer experience. This means empowering them to take initiative and providing them with the tools and training they need to be proactive problem solvers.

Encouraging a Proactive Mindset

Your team needs to understand the importance of being proactive and how it benefits both the customer and the business. Begin by sharing real-world examples of how proactive service has led to positive outcomes, whether from your own business or from other companies. Make it clear that their role isn't just to respond to customer issues but to anticipate and prevent those issues from arising in the first place. Proactive service builds customer loyalty, improves satisfaction, and can even reduce the workload by addressing common problems before they escalate.

Encourage your team to slow down and notice patterns in customer interactions. Are your customer service representatives noticing the same questions or concerns coming up repeatedly in calls or emails? Are account managers hearing similar feedback from multiple customers? Identifying these recurring themes allows your team to address the root causes and implement solutions proactively.

By fostering a proactive mindset within your team, you empower them to go beyond reactive problem-solving. Encourage them to take initiative, offer solutions before customers need to ask, and look for ways to make the customer experience smoother at every touchpoint.

Empowering Employees to Take Action

Proactive service requires giving your employees the authority to make decisions and solve problems without constantly needing approval from management. For example, if a customer is unhappy with a service delay, empower your employees to offer a discount, a free product, or free shipping without escalating the issue. This not only speeds up the resolution process but also shows customers that your team is committed to making things right on the spot.

Chapter 3: Proactive vs. Reactive Service

The key to this is trust. You need to trust your employees to act in the best interest of the customer and the company. Allow and encourage them to remediate situations themselves. If an employee breaks that trust, the issue should be addressed with the employee—not at the expense of your customers. Use such instances as opportunities to refine your processes, implement better checks and balances, and increase visibility and tracking. However, never strip your employees of their ability to take action and resolve customer issues directly. This empowerment is what makes proactive service possible and effective.

Recognizing and Rewarding Proactivity

To reinforce a proactive culture, recognize and reward employees who go above and beyond to prevent issues or create positive experiences for customers. Whether through public recognition, bonuses, or other incentives, showing that you value proactive behavior encourages more of it across the team.

For example, if an employee notices that a customer's order will be delayed due to a backlog with your preferred shipper but takes the initiative to use an alternative shipping service to get the product delivered on time, even if it costs a little more, that employee should be rewarded for going the extra mile for the customer. Their proactive action not only avoids a negative customer experience but also demonstrates a commitment to **Service First**.

Even small rewards for proactive behavior can have a big impact. At the end of the year, you can enter all employees who were recognized for putting **Service First** into a drawing for a significant reward, such as an additional week of PTO, a $1,000 cash bonus, or another high-value prize. This type of incentive motivates employees to go above and beyond in hopes of being recognized, while also reinforcing a culture where customer care is prioritized.

When your employees feel valued and appreciated for their efforts to go above and beyond for customers, they will, in turn, go above and beyond for your business.

Tools and Systems for Monitoring Customer Satisfaction

Proactive service also requires constant monitoring of customer satisfaction so that you can identify issues before they become major problems. There are several tools and systems that can help you stay ahead of customer concerns:

- **Surveys and Feedback Forms**: Regularly ask your customers for feedback through post-purchase surveys, satisfaction forms, or product reviews. This allows you to catch any issues early and address them before they escalate. Actively review this feedback to spot any patterns that may indicate a broader problem.

- **Social Media Monitoring**: Keep an eye on what customers are saying about your business on social media. If you notice a trend of complaints or negative comments, address the underlying issue proactively.

Remember, don't censor negative comments or reviews. Instead, use them as an opportunity to resolve the issue publicly. Refer to the L.A.S.T. method, explained in the next section, to handle these situations effectively.

- **Customer Support Data**: Analyze your customer support interactions to identify recurring issues. If you notice a spike in complaints about a particular service or product, investigate why it's happening and find a solution before it affects more customers.

- **CRM Tools**: Use customer relationship management (CRM) tools to track customer interactions, preferences, and past issues. This data helps you anticipate future needs, allowing you to offer more personalized service and proactively address potential concerns.

Handling Customer Complaints Effectively

Even with a proactive approach, there will still be times when things go wrong. The key to handling complaints effectively is to respond quickly, empathetically, and with a solution-oriented mindset. In a **Service First** business, complaints are seen as opportunities to strengthen customer relationships, not just problems to be fixed.

Turning Complaints into Opportunities

When a customer complains, they're giving you valuable insight into what went wrong and how you can improve. Instead of viewing complaints as negative feedback, see them as opportunities to exceed the customer's expectations.

One method that was taught to me—and regularly engrained in my approach—is called **"L.A.S.T."** This method is simple, easy to understand, and just as easy to implement:

1. **Listen**:
   When a customer makes a complaint, give them your full attention. Let them explain the issue without interrupting, and make sure they feel heard. Active listening is key here—repeating back or summarizing what the customer said can reassure them that you fully understand their concern.

2. **Apologize**:
   Acknowledge the customer's frustration and express understanding. A simple, sincere apology like, "I'm sorry that happened," can go a long way in making the customer feel valued. It shows empathy and helps diffuse frustration.

3. **Solve**:
   Offer a solution that goes beyond the customer's expectations. Whether it's a refund, replacement, or a special offer, ensure the customer leaves the interaction feeling satisfied and appreciated. Make it clear that you are committed to making things right.

4. **Thank**:
   Finally, thank the customer for bringing the issue to your attention. They took time out of their day to help you improve, and their feedback is valuable. A simple thank-you reinforces that you value their time and effort.

Example of the L.A.S.T. Method in Action

Let's say a customer orders a product from your e-commerce store and it arrives damaged. They reach out to your support team, clearly frustrated because they needed the item for an upcoming event. Here's how you could apply the L.A.S.T. method:

1. **Listen**:
   The customer explains that they received the product damaged and that they needed it for a family gathering in three days. Your support agent listens attentively, without interrupting, and asks clarifying questions like, "Can you tell me more about the damage?" The agent ensures the customer feels heard by summarizing the situation: "I understand you needed the product for your event this weekend, and it arrived damaged. I can see how frustrating this must be."

2. **Apologize**:
   The agent offers a sincere apology: "I'm really sorry that the item arrived damaged, especially when you needed it for such an important event. I completely understand your frustration, and we'll work to make this right."

3. **Solve**:
   The agent then presents a solution that exceeds the customer's expectations: "To make sure you have the item in time, I'll expedite a replacement at no additional charge and have it shipped overnight to ensure it arrives before your event. Additionally, we'd like to offer you a 15% discount on your next purchase as a gesture of goodwill for the inconvenience."

4. **Thank**:
   After confirming the replacement has been arranged, the agent thanks the customer: "I really appreciate you bringing this to our attention and giving us the opportunity to make it right. Thank you for your patience, and please don't hesitate to reach out if there's anything else we can do."

By applying the **L.A.S.T.** method, not only does the customer's frustration get resolved, but they also leave the interaction feeling valued and satisfied. They're more likely to remember how well the situation was handled and may even recommend your business to others despite the initial issue.

Summary

In this chapter we explored the power of proactive service and its role in building trust and loyalty with customers. By anticipating customer needs and addressing potential issues before they arise, businesses can prevent negative experiences and enhance customer satisfaction.

A key takeaway from this chapter is the importance of empowering employees to make decisions and solve problems without waiting for approval from management. When employees are trusted to handle customer concerns on the spot — whether that means offering discounts, resolving issues, or providing additional support — it not only speeds up resolutions but also creates a positive, customer-centric culture.

Chapter 3: Proactive vs. Reactive Service

We also discussed how to foster a proactive mindset within your team. This involves encouraging employees to look for patterns in customer feedback, complaints, and support interactions to address recurring issues before they escalate. Using tools like customer relationship management (CRM) systems, customer surveys, and social media monitoring helps you stay ahead of potential problems and continuously improve the customer experience.

Lastly, the chapter covered effective complaint handling using the **L.A.S.T.** method: **Listen**, **Apologize**, **Solve**, and **Thank**. Complaints should be viewed as opportunities to exceed customer expectations and strengthen relationships. By responding quickly, empathetically, and with a solution-oriented mindset, businesses can turn negative experiences into positive ones and build long-lasting trust.

This chapter underscores that proactive service, empowered employees, and thoughtful handling of complaints are key components of a **Service First** approach that drives customer loyalty and business success.

Exercises

Exercise 1: Anticipating Customer Needs

This exercise helps you identify patterns in customer interactions and anticipate common issues before they arise.

Steps:

1. **Analyze your customer feedback**: Review recent customer feedback, support requests, and common questions. Look for recurring issues or patterns that suggest areas where customers may be struggling.

2. **Identify 2-3 potential problems** that customers might face based on your findings (e.g., frequent delays in a specific product, confusion about a process).

3. **Develop a proactive solution**: For each identified problem, create a plan to address it before it escalates. This could be a preemptive communication (e.g., an email explaining how to use a product) or an internal process change (e.g., improving your shipping procedures to avoid delays).

4. **Implement one solution**: Choose one of the proactive solutions and implement it in your business. Track the results and customer feedback over the next month to see how effective it is.

Exercise 2: Empowering Employees to Take Action

Empowering employees to make decisions is a key part of providing proactive service. This exercise will help you evaluate your current policies and find ways to give your team more authority.

Steps:

1. **Evaluate your current policies**: Review your current processes for handling customer complaints and issues. Do employees need approval to offer solutions (e.g., refunds, discounts)? How often are issues escalated to management?

2. **Identify 2 areas** where employees could be empowered to resolve customer issues without needing approval (e.g., offering a free replacement for damaged goods or providing expedited shipping for delayed orders).

3. **Set guidelines**: Create a clear framework for employees, including what they're authorized to do and when they should escalate an issue. The goal is to empower them while ensuring consistency in customer service.

4. **Role-play scenarios**: Conduct a role-playing session with your team, presenting them with common customer issues. Have them practice responding using the guidelines you've created, allowing them to make decisions on their own.

Exercise 3: Handling Complaints with the L.A.S.T. Method

The **L.A.S.T.** method is crucial for turning negative situations into positive customer experiences. This exercise will help you practice and reinforce this method.

Steps:

1. **Review a recent complaint**: Think of a recent customer complaint your business received. How was it handled? Could the issue have been resolved more effectively?

2. **Apply the L.A.S.T. method**: Break down how the complaint could have been handled using the **L.A.S.T.** method:

    - **Listen**: Were you or your team fully attentive to the customer's concerns?
    - **Apologize**: Did you offer a genuine apology that acknowledged the customer's frustration?
    - **Solve**: Was the solution offered something that exceeded the customer's expectations?

- o **Thank**: Did you thank the customer for their time and feedback?

3. **Write a response**: Draft a response using the **L.A.S.T.** method for a hypothetical customer complaint. Practice delivering the response either via email or in a live role-play situation with a colleague.

4. **Reflection**: How did the response feel compared to previous ways of handling complaints? How do you think the customer would feel if they received this level of attention and care?

Exercise 4: Monitoring Customer Satisfaction

Constantly monitoring customer satisfaction helps catch issues before they escalate. This exercise will help you set up and refine your monitoring system.

Steps:

1. **Set up feedback channels**: Ensure you have mechanisms in place to regularly gather customer feedback (e.g., post-purchase surveys, satisfaction forms, or product reviews).

2. **Choose a tool**: Select a tool to monitor customer feedback and satisfaction (e.g., CRM software, social media monitoring, or customer support analytics).

3. **Analyze recent data**: Review the past month of customer feedback or support interactions. Identify any recurring issues that customers are facing.

4. **Create an action plan**: Based on your analysis, create a plan to proactively address any common issues you've discovered. For example, if several customers mentioned

difficulty navigating your website, consider redesigning the layout to improve usability.

Exercise 5: Rewarding Proactive Behavior

Recognizing and rewarding employees who go above and beyond helps reinforce a proactive culture. This exercise will help you set up a system for recognizing employee contributions.

Steps:

1. **Review recent employee actions**: Think about times when your employees took proactive steps to improve customer service or solve a problem. Were they recognized for their efforts?

2. **Establish recognition criteria**: Define what proactive behaviors you want to reward (e.g., resolving customer issues without escalation, anticipating and addressing problems before they occur).

3. **Create a recognition program**: Set up a system to regularly recognize and reward employees who demonstrate proactive service. This could be public recognition, small bonuses, or other incentives.

4. **Implement your system**: Put your recognition program into place. Track how it affects employee behavior and customer satisfaction over the next quarter.

Exercise 6: Leveraging Technology for Proactive Service

Technology plays a major role in delivering proactive service. This exercise will help you identify areas where you can use tools to improve customer interactions.

Steps:

1. **Evaluate your current technology**: Look at the tools you're currently using (e.g., CRM systems, email marketing platforms, social media monitoring). Are there gaps in how you're using these tools to anticipate customer needs?

2. **Choose one area**: Identify one area where technology could help you be more proactive. For example, could you use automated follow-up emails to check in with customers after a purchase or use CRM data to anticipate when a customer might need support?

3. **Implement a new tool or feature**: Set up an automated workflow or integrate a new feature into your system that allows you to stay one step ahead of customer needs.

4. **Monitor the results**: After implementing the tool or feature, track how it impacts customer satisfaction and whether it helps you address issues proactively.

Chapter 3: Proactive vs. Reactive Service

Chapter 4: Personalizing the Customer Experience

In today's market, customers expect more than just a one-size-fits-all approach. Personalization has become a key driver of customer satisfaction, loyalty, and overall experience. Businesses that take the time to understand their customers' unique needs and preferences are better positioned to create meaningful connections and deliver more value. In a **Service First** business, personalization isn't just a nice-to-have; it's an essential part of creating a customer-centric experience.

When you personalize your service, you show your customers that they are more than just a transaction. You acknowledge their individuality, which makes them feel appreciated and valued. This chapter explores the importance of personalizing the customer experience, practical ways to tailor interactions, and how doing so can significantly improve customer loyalty.

Knowing Your Customer Personally

To offer personalized service, you need to start with a deep understanding of your customer. Who are they? What are their preferences, challenges, and needs? Getting to know your customers personally is key to delivering service that feels tailored to them.

The Power of Personalization

Personalization is a powerful tool because it goes beyond offering generic service. When you tailor your interactions to meet an individual's specific needs, customers feel understood and appreciated. This extra effort translates into loyalty, repeat business, and a stronger connection to your brand.

Consider this example: a customer walks into your store and is greeted by name because they've shopped there before. The sales associate remembers their previous purchase and offers a recommendation based on their preferences. This personal touch makes the customer feel seen and valued, creating a positive experience that makes them more likely to return.

In contrast, an impersonal experience — where the customer feels like just another face in the crowd — leaves little lasting impression. The more you personalize, the more your business stands out and becomes memorable to your customers.

Another example is when someone presents a ticket at an event. When their ticket is scanned, their name appears, and they're greeted with a personal message like, "Thank you for coming tonight, Mr. Smith. I hope you enjoy the show!" or "Welcome, Ms. Jackson! You should try our new restaurant by the Ferris wheel; the food there is my favorite." These small, personalized interactions show that you care about each customer as an individual, enhancing their overall experience.

Gathering Customer Insights

To personalize the customer experience, you need to gather insights about your customers. This can be done in a number of ways, including:

- **Customer Data**: Collecting information through past purchases, preferences, and behavior. CRM tools can help track this data over time.

- **Surveys and Feedback**: Regularly ask your customers for their opinions and preferences. Simple surveys can provide valuable insights into what they like, don't like, or would like to see in the future.

- **Direct Conversations**: Sometimes, the best way to learn about your customer is to ask directly. Engaging in conversations with customers gives you a deeper understanding of their needs and desires.

Using Data Wisely

It's important to use the customer data you collect responsibly. Personalization should feel helpful, not intrusive. There's a fine line between offering a tailored experience and making the customer feel like their privacy has been violated. Always be transparent about how you use customer information, and ensure you're providing real value in return for the data you collect.

For example, sending a personalized discount based on past purchases feels thoughtful and useful, but bombarding a customer with overly specific ads based on every action they take can come across as invasive.

A well-known example of crossing this line occurred in 2012 when Target (a major U.S. department store) used predictive analytics to determine that a teen girl was pregnant before her family knew. Target proactively sent baby-related coupons to her home, which led her father to angrily confront the store, as he had no idea she was expecting. After talking to his daughter, the father later apologized, realizing Target's prediction was correct. However, this situation felt "creepy" to many because the personalization was too specific and invasive.

The key is to **be helpful, not creepy**. For instance, if you collect customers' birthdays to verify their eligibility for your products or services, sending them a birthday card or discount via email or regular mail can be a nice touch. However, showing up at their house to hand-deliver a card or present would likely cross the line into feeling invasive.

Lastly, ensure you have a clear privacy policy and that you follow it. Transparency about how you use customer data builds trust, while respecting their privacy ensures that personalization feels appropriate and valuable.

Small Touches, Big Impact

Personalization doesn't have to be complex or expensive. Small touches can have a big impact when done right. Even simple gestures that make customers feel special can create a lasting impression.

Here are some examples of small ways to personalize the customer experience:

- **Using Names**: Addressing your customers by name—whether in person, in emails, or over the phone—

immediately makes the interaction feel more personal. A customer is more likely to respond positively when they hear or see their own name. In e-commerce, for example, an email that begins with "Dear John Smith..." feels more personal and engaging than a generic greeting.

- **Customized Offers**: Tailoring promotions or discounts based on a customer's past behavior or preferences shows that you're paying attention to their needs. For instance, if a customer frequently purchases a particular type of product, offering a discount on a related item demonstrates that you understand their interests. If you sell a similar product, recommending it as their next purchase adds an extra layer of personalization.

- **Remembering Preferences**: Whether it's a customer's favorite drink at a coffee shop or the specific services they prefer, remembering and catering to their preferences enhances their experience. Small gestures like this show customers that you value their individuality and are committed to delivering a personalized experience.

- **Follow-Up After Purchase**: Personalizing the post-purchase experience can also make a big difference. Following up to ask how a customer is enjoying their purchase, offering tips to maximize the product's use, or checking in to see if they need any help shows that you care about their long-term satisfaction.

Tailoring Your Service Approach

Not all customers are the same, so it's important to offer flexibility in your service approach. Tailoring your service to meet the specific needs and preferences of different customers creates a more meaningful and impactful experience.

Segmenting Your Customer Base

A great way to tailor your service is by segmenting your customer base into groups with similar characteristics or needs. Some customers may prioritize speed and efficiency, while others value personalized attention and detailed service. By understanding these different segments, you can adjust your approach to suit their specific preferences.

Here are some examples:

- **High-Touch Customers**: These customers prefer a lot of interaction and attention. They appreciate detailed explanations, one-on-one consultations, and follow-up communication. Offering a more personalized service to these customers—such as dedicated support or tailored recommendations—makes them feel valued and understood.

- **Self-Service Customers**: These customers prefer a more hands-off approach, where they can navigate your products or services independently. For them, it's essential to provide tools, resources, and information that allow them to find what they need without extensive interaction. A well-designed website, detailed FAQs, and self-help options are key to satisfying this customer segment.

By recognizing these differences, you can adjust your service style to match the preferences of each customer segment, ensuring that all customers feel comfortable and satisfied with their experience.

Additionally, you can segment customers further based on factors such as industry, geographical location, or purchasing behavior. A CRM system will allow you to easily track and manage this information, helping you implement personalized strategies that resonate with each customer group.

Providing Custom Solutions

Another way to tailor your service is by offering custom solutions that fit the unique needs of individual customers. Instead of providing a one-size-fits-all answer, consider how you can adapt your products or services to better meet the specific circumstances of each customer.

For example, a customer might need a product or service slightly modified to suit their requirements. Being flexible and accommodating these requests — when feasible — can transform a standard transaction into a memorable, personalized experience. Customers appreciate businesses that go the extra mile to address their unique needs.

The **Service First** approach can start early in the process, depending on your type of business. For instance, if your business involves pre-sales consultations or on-site visits for estimates, this is a great opportunity to learn more about what the customer is trying to achieve. You can use this interaction to clarify what the customer is looking for and potentially offer solutions they hadn't considered.

In my case, if I understand what a customer is trying to accomplish, I can suggest hardware options that might better fit their business needs than what we currently have in stock. Offering custom servers that align with their specific needs ensures greater customer satisfaction and a more tailored service experience.

Personalization in the Digital Age

With advancements in technology, it's easier than ever to personalize interactions with customers. However, the key is to find a balance between automation and maintaining a human touch.

Leveraging Technology for Personalization

Today's CRM tools, email marketing platforms, and e-commerce systems allow you to collect and use data in ways that enhance the customer experience. For instance, many businesses use:

- **Email Personalization**: Sending targeted emails that address customers by name and recommend products based on their previous purchases or browsing behavior. Personalized emails can feel more relevant to the recipient and are more likely to be opened and acted upon.

- **Dynamic Content on Websites**: E-commerce platforms and websites can offer personalized experiences by showing customers products or services based on their past behavior. For example, an online store might feature items similar to what the customer has already viewed or purchased, making their shopping experience smoother and more enjoyable.

- **Automated Messaging**: Automated systems can send follow-up messages or notifications based on specific customer actions, such as abandoning a shopping cart or completing a purchase. These messages can include personalized offers, reminders, or customer support options, all aimed at improving the overall experience.

While these tools are powerful, it's important to maintain the human touch wherever possible. Technology should support personalized service, but not replace the genuine, one-on-one interactions that make customers feel truly valued. Automated systems can be great for efficiency, but they should always leave room for real, human responses when needed.

Balancing Automation and Human Interaction

In a **Service First** business, it's essential to strike the right balance between using technology for personalization and keeping interactions personal. While automation can streamline processes and make it easier to provide timely service, human interaction adds warmth, empathy, and understanding to the customer experience.

When to Use Automation

Automation works best for repetitive tasks that don't require a personal touch. For example, sending order confirmations, shipping updates, or reminders can be automated without sacrificing the customer experience. Automation can also be helpful for gathering initial customer information or sending out general surveys and feedback forms.

When to Stay Personal

However, when it comes to resolving issues, handling complaints, or dealing with more complex inquiries, a personal approach is always better. Customers value speaking to a real person who understands their concerns and can offer genuine empathy. Even if you use automation to trigger follow-ups or reminders, make sure there's a way for customers to easily reach a human representative when they need more detailed assistance.

Blending Automation with Personalization

You don't have to choose between automation and human interaction — both can work together to create a seamless customer experience. For example, you can use automation to send a personalized follow-up email after a customer makes a purchase, while also offering them the option to contact a representative directly if they need further assistance. This blend of technology and human interaction allows you to provide fast, efficient service without sacrificing the personal touch.

In another example, at my company, customers can open support tickets by simply sending an email to our help desk. To ensure they know their message was received, I've set up an automated response that confirms the ticket has been created and that someone will respond shortly. The next response, however, always comes from a human. This way, customers benefit from the speed of automation while still receiving the personal attention they need.

Turning Personalization into Loyalty

Ultimately, personalizing the customer experience is about building relationships. When customers feel like a business understands them — whether through remembering their preferences, offering tailored solutions, or providing thoughtful follow-ups — they develop a sense of loyalty. Personalization strengthens the connection between your business and your customers, making them more likely to return and recommend your business to others.

Building Trust Through Personalization

Personalized service shows customers that you value them as individuals. By acknowledging their specific needs and preferences, you demonstrate that their business matters to you. This builds trust, which is the foundation of any long-term customer relationship. Customers who feel understood and appreciated are far more likely to remain loyal, even in competitive markets.

Creating Repeat Customers

Repeat customers are the backbone of any successful business. Personalizing the customer experience helps turn one-time buyers into lifelong customers by making each interaction feel unique and valuable. When customers know that they'll receive individualized attention every time they interact with your business, they'll be more inclined to return for future purchases or services.

Summary

Personalizing the customer experience is a powerful way to differentiate your business and build lasting relationships with your customers. By getting to know your customers, using small personal touches, and tailoring your service approach to meet their specific needs, you create a more meaningful and enjoyable experience. Leveraging technology to enhance personalization, while maintaining the human touch, ensures that your customers feel valued at every stage of their journey.

In a **Service First** business, personalization isn't just about providing a better customer experience—it's about building trust, loyalty, and long-term success. By making your customers feel seen, understood, and appreciated, you'll turn everyday interactions into memorable experiences that keep them coming back.

Exercises

Exercise 1: Personalizing Customer Interactions

This exercise helps you incorporate personalization into customer interactions, making them feel more valued and recognized.

Steps:

1. **Identify touchpoints**: List the key points in your customer journey where personalization could make an impact (e.g., greeting customers by name, personalized follow-up emails, or recommendations based on past purchases).

2. **Implement a simple change**: Choose one touchpoint and implement a personalized element. For example, add a customer's name to email communications or remember and mention a customer's preferences during interactions.

3. **Measure the impact**: After making the change, observe customer reactions. Do customers respond more positively? Track any improvements in engagement, satisfaction, or feedback.

Exercise 2: Segmenting Your Customer Base

Segmenting your customers allows you to tailor services to meet their specific needs. This exercise will help you start segmenting your customer base.

Steps:

1. **Analyze your customer base**: Identify common characteristics that differentiate your customers (e.g., preferences for high-touch service vs. self-service, industry type, location).

2. **Create customer segments**: Group your customers into 2-3 segments based on similar needs or behaviors (e.g., high-touch customers who prefer one-on-one attention and self-service customers who prefer minimal interaction).

3. **Tailor your service**: Develop one or two ways to adjust your service approach for each segment. For example, create a dedicated support channel for high-touch customers and provide more self-help resources for self-service customers.

4. **Track results**: After tailoring your service, monitor customer satisfaction and feedback to see how your adjustments impact each segment.

Exercise 3: Offering Customized Solutions

This exercise encourages you to practice offering custom solutions that meet individual customer needs.

Steps:

1. **Review recent customer requests**: Identify recent customer interactions where you could have provided a more customized solution (e.g., product modifications, personalized recommendations).

2. **Brainstorm custom options**: Think of ways you could modify or adapt your products or services to better meet the specific needs of these customers. Consider whether flexibility in pricing, features, or delivery options would improve their experience.

3. **Offer a custom solution**: Next time a customer needs something slightly different, offer a custom solution tailored to their needs. Document how the customer responds and whether this leads to increased satisfaction or loyalty.

Exercise 4: Balancing Automation and Human Interaction

Automation can improve efficiency, but combining it with human interaction creates a better customer experience. This exercise helps you strike that balance.

Steps:

1. **Identify areas for automation**: Look at your current customer service processes. Where could automation improve efficiency without sacrificing the personal touch (e.g., automated order confirmations, follow-up emails, or support ticket acknowledgments)?

2. **Set up automation**: Implement automation in one part of your process (e.g., an automated email response that confirms a customer's inquiry was received).

3. **Add a personal touch**: Ensure that the next customer interaction is handled by a person. For example, follow up the automated message with a personalized response from a team member.

4. **Evaluate customer responses**: After blending automation with human interaction, monitor customer feedback. Are they satisfied with the level of service? Does this improve your team's efficiency?

Exercise 5: Using Data to Personalize Service

Collecting and using customer data effectively helps you offer a more personalized experience. This exercise helps you use data responsibly while tailoring your service.

Steps:

1. **Review the data you collect**: Identify the types of customer data you currently collect (e.g., purchase history, preferences, demographics). Is this data used to improve personalization?

2. **Find one area to apply personalization**: Choose one type of data and use it to personalize your service. For

instance, offer a discount on a product that complements a previous purchase, or send birthday messages with special offers if you track customer birthdays.

3. **Monitor customer responses**: Pay attention to how customers respond to these personalized touches. Do they engage more or show increased satisfaction when their service is tailored to them?

4. **Ensure transparency**: Make sure customers are aware of how their data is being used. Review your privacy policy and communication to ensure customers feel comfortable and informed about how their information is handled.

Exercise 6: Follow-Up After Purchase

Following up after a purchase is a simple yet powerful way to enhance the customer experience. This exercise helps you implement follow-ups that make a difference.

Steps:

1. **Choose a follow-up method**: Identify a method for following up with customers after their purchase (e.g., a thank-you email, product tips, or a satisfaction survey).

2. **Create a follow-up template**: Write a follow-up message that includes personalized elements, such as addressing the customer by name and offering support based on their specific purchase (e.g., "Here are some tips to get the most out of your new product…").

3. **Implement the follow-up**: Send the follow-up message to customers within a set period after their purchase (e.g., 3-7 days).

4. **Track customer responses**: Measure the impact of follow-ups on customer satisfaction, repeat purchases, or feedback. Note any areas where personalization could further enhance the follow-up process.

Chapter 4: Personalizing the Customer Experience

Chapter 5: Building Long-Term Relationships with Customers

Creating strong, long-lasting relationships with your customers is one of the most valuable outcomes of a **Service First** approach. While winning new customers is important, cultivating long-term loyalty is essential for sustainable success. Loyal customers are more likely to return, refer others, and become ambassadors for your brand, saving you the high costs of constantly acquiring new customers.

In this chapter, we'll explore the value of customer loyalty, practical strategies to build lasting relationships, and how to consistently deliver on your **Service First** promise to keep customers coming back for more.

The Value of Loyalty

Customer loyalty doesn't just happen. It's the result of continuous effort to provide a positive, reliable, and valuable experience. In a competitive marketplace, where customers can easily switch to a different brand or service, loyalty is an asset that sets you apart.

Why Loyal Customers Are More Valuable

Loyal customers offer more than just repeat business — they provide stability and long-term growth. Here's why they are so valuable:

- **Lower Acquisition Costs**: It's far more expensive to acquire a new customer than to retain an existing one. Loyal customers reduce your need to spend heavily on marketing and sales.

- **Higher Lifetime Value**: A loyal customer tends to spend more over time. They trust your business, are more willing to purchase higher-priced items, and are less likely to be influenced by competitors.

- **Word-of-Mouth Referrals**: Happy, loyal customers often become your best advocates. They recommend your business to friends, family, and colleagues, driving new business through personal referrals — arguably the most powerful form of marketing.

When customers feel connected to your business, they stick around. They are more forgiving when things go wrong and are more likely to give you the benefit of the doubt when facing issues. This loyalty isn't built overnight, but through consistent, positive interactions that make them feel valued.

Strategies for Building Customer Loyalty

Building customer loyalty isn't about one grand gesture — it's about a series of small, thoughtful actions that demonstrate you care about your customers and are committed to their satisfaction. Here are some strategies to help cultivate long-term relationships:

1. Consistent Communication

Staying in touch with your customers helps keep your business top of mind and fosters a sense of connection. However, communication must be thoughtful and relevant—it's not about bombarding your customers with sales pitches but rather providing value through regular, meaningful interactions.

- **Personalized Follow-Ups**: After a purchase or service, follow up with your customers to check on their satisfaction. This could be as simple as an email or phone call thanking them for their business and asking if there's anything else you can help with. Personalized follow-ups make customers feel appreciated and show that you care about their experience.

- **Regular Updates**: Keep your customers informed about new products, services, or special offers. Regular updates—through newsletters, social media, or emails—give your customers a reason to stay engaged with your brand.

2. Rewarding Loyalty

Loyalty programs are a tried-and-true method of rewarding repeat customers and incentivizing them to keep coming back. However, your loyalty program doesn't need to be complex to be effective. The goal is to show your customers that you recognize and appreciate their continued business.

- **Exclusive Discounts**: Offering exclusive deals or discounts to loyal customers is a great way to reward them for their loyalty. Whether it's a percentage off their next purchase or early access to new products, customers love feeling like they're part of an "inner circle."

- **Referral Incentives**: Encourage loyal customers to refer new business by offering incentives such as discounts or

Chapter 5: Building Long-Term Relationships with Customers

rewards for successful referrals. This not only brings in new customers but also strengthens the bond with your existing customer base.

3. Exceeding Expectations

Customers expect a certain level of service from businesses, but exceeding those expectations is what turns a one-time customer into a loyal one. Whether it's through going the extra mile or delivering a surprise element of value, exceeding expectations leaves a lasting impression.

- **Surprise Perks**: Offering unexpected perks — like a free upgrade, a small gift, or a hand-written thank-you note — can create a memorable experience that makes customers feel special and appreciated.

- **Anticipating Needs**: Proactively solving a problem or addressing a need before the customer even brings it up demonstrates that you're truly paying attention. This proactive approach shows customers that you're not just fulfilling their current needs but are also thinking ahead about how to better serve them.

4. Providing Exceptional Support

How you handle customer issues, complaints, and questions can make or break a relationship. Even when things go wrong, providing exceptional support and resolving issues quickly can actually strengthen customer loyalty.

- **Quick and Empathetic Responses**: When customers reach out with a problem, your response time and the quality of your communication matter. The faster you can resolve the issue, and the more empathy you show, the better the outcome. Apologize for any inconvenience, offer a solution, and make sure the customer leaves the interaction feeling valued.

- **Follow Up After Issues Are Resolved**: Don't just resolve the issue and move on—take the extra step of following up with the customer to ensure they're fully satisfied. This small gesture shows that you care about their experience beyond the initial problem.

Turning Transactions into Relationships

Customers today expect more than just a transactional relationship with businesses. They want to feel connected, valued, and appreciated. In a **Service First** business, your goal is to transform each interaction into a building block of a long-term relationship.

Building Trust Through Consistency

Consistency is one of the most important factors in building trust with your customers. If customers know they can rely on you to deliver a consistently positive experience—whether through on-time deliveries, accurate orders, or responsive customer service—they will trust you. Trust is the foundation of any strong relationship, and it's earned through reliability and consistency.

Creating Emotional Connections

Customers don't just stay loyal to businesses because of good products or services—they stay because of the emotional connection they feel with the brand. By providing personalized service, anticipating their needs, and making them feel valued, you create an emotional bond that goes beyond the transactional nature of business.

Consider how you can make your customers feel seen and appreciated. Small gestures—like remembering their name, sending a thank-you note, or offering a surprise discount—help build an emotional connection that keeps them coming back.

Follow-Ups and Post-Service Care

Once a transaction is complete, your job isn't done. One of the most overlooked aspects of customer service is post-service care—how you interact with customers after the sale or service is over. This follow-up can strengthen the relationship and keep customers coming back.

The Importance of Checking In

Following up with customers after they've made a purchase or used your service shows that you're invested in their satisfaction beyond the initial transaction. It also gives you an opportunity to address any issues before they escalate and gather feedback on how you can improve.

- **Simple Thank-Yous**: A simple thank-you email or message can go a long way in showing customers that you appreciate their business. Personalizing the message adds an extra layer of sincerity.

- **Surveys and Feedback Requests**: Ask customers for feedback on their experience, whether through a quick survey or direct outreach. Not only does this help you improve, but it also shows customers that you value their opinion.

Creating Lifelong Customers

Building loyalty doesn't end with the first follow-up. Lifelong customers are created through a continuous cycle of engagement, appreciation, and service. The more consistently you follow up and provide value after the initial transaction, the more likely customers are to remain loyal.

Summary

Building long-term relationships with your customers is essential for the sustainable growth of your business. By fostering loyalty through consistent communication, rewarding repeat business, exceeding expectations, and providing exceptional support, you turn one-time buyers into lifelong customers. A **Service First** approach prioritizes creating strong, lasting connections that build trust and emotional bonds, ensuring that your customers feel valued and appreciated at every step of their journey with your business.

In the next chapter, we'll dive into the challenges of scaling customer service as your business grows and how to maintain high service standards while expanding your customer base.

Exercises

Exercise 1: Understanding Your Customer's Journey

To build long-term relationships, you need to understand your customers' journey with your business. This exercise helps you identify key touchpoints where relationships are developed and maintained.

Steps:

1. **Map out the customer journey**: Identify key stages in your customer's experience with your business, from initial discovery to post-purchase follow-up. This includes marketing, sales, onboarding, and ongoing support.

2. **Identify relationship-building opportunities**: At each stage, list specific opportunities to strengthen the relationship. For example, offering onboarding support after a purchase or sending personalized follow-ups.

3. **Improve a touchpoint**: Choose one stage where you think your customer relationship could be improved (e.g., post-purchase follow-up) and implement a change to make it more personalized or engaging.

4. **Track the impact**: After improving the touchpoint, monitor customer feedback or behavior to see if it strengthens their connection with your business.

Exercise 2: Creating a Customer Loyalty Program

Customer loyalty programs are effective in fostering long-term relationships. This exercise will guide you in creating a loyalty program that rewards repeat customers.

Steps:

1. **Review your repeat customers**: Analyze your customer data to identify customers who return frequently. What products or services do they tend to buy? What keeps them coming back?

2. **Design a loyalty program**: Create a simple loyalty program that rewards repeat customers. For example, you could offer discounts after a certain number of purchases, exclusive early access to new products, or personalized rewards based on their preferences.

3. **Launch the program**: Introduce the loyalty program to a select group of customers or through a small pilot

program. Make sure the program is easy to understand and rewarding for your customers.

4. **Evaluate success**: After launching the program, track how many customers engage with it and whether it leads to more repeat business.

Exercise 3: Personalizing Customer Communication

This exercise helps you build long-term relationships by improving personalized communication with customers.

Steps:

1. **Review past communications**: Look at recent emails, messages, or other communications sent to customers. How personal were these interactions? Did you address the customer by name? Were the messages relevant to their interests or needs?

2. **Create personalized communication**: For your next round of communication (e.g., email newsletter, follow-up calls), personalize the message for individual customers. Use their name, refer to their past purchases, and offer relevant content or suggestions based on their preferences.

3. **Track engagement**: After sending the personalized messages, monitor how customers respond. Are they more engaged? Do they interact more with the content or offer positive feedback?

4. **Iterate**: Use the results to continuously improve your communication strategy, ensuring that each customer feels recognized and valued.

Chapter 5: Building Long-Term Relationships with Customers

Exercise 4: Building Trust Through Transparency

Trust is the foundation of long-term relationships. This exercise helps you improve transparency in your business practices.

Steps:

1. **Review your current transparency efforts**: Evaluate how transparent your business is with customers in areas like pricing, policies, and service delivery. Are there any areas where customers might feel uncertain or misled?

2. **Improve one area of transparency**: Choose one area where you can improve transparency. For example, make your pricing more clear by outlining any additional fees upfront, or improve communication about potential service delays.

3. **Communicate clearly with customers**: Update your messaging to reflect this improved transparency. For example, create a FAQ section or send proactive emails outlining important details that could affect customers.

4. **Monitor customer feedback**: After making the changes, track customer reactions. Are they more trusting and appreciative of the transparent communication?

Exercise 5: Providing Value Beyond Transactions

Building long-term relationships requires offering value beyond just the initial purchase. This exercise helps you focus on how to provide lasting value to your customers.

Steps:

1. **Identify value-added services**: Think about how your business can provide ongoing value beyond just selling a

product or service. For example, this could be offering free resources, industry insights, exclusive content, or regular check-ins to ensure the customer is satisfied.

2. **Create a post-purchase strategy**: Develop a plan for keeping in touch with customers after a purchase. This could include sending tips on how to get the most out of their purchase, providing follow-up support, or inviting them to exclusive events or webinars.

3. **Implement the strategy**: Put your post-purchase strategy into action. Make sure it's consistent, engaging, and adds value for your customers.

4. **Measure long-term engagement**: Track how often customers return to engage with your business after the initial transaction. If engagement increases, it's a sign that you're providing ongoing value and building a lasting relationship.

Exercise 6: Handling Complaints to Strengthen Relationships

How you handle complaints plays a significant role in building long-term relationships. This exercise focuses on turning complaints into opportunities to improve customer relationships.

Steps:

1. **Review recent customer complaints**: Identify any recent complaints that were handled by your team. Were these interactions resolved to the customer's satisfaction? Did you follow up to ensure the customer felt valued?

2. **Develop a complaint resolution plan**: Create a standard process for handling complaints that includes active

listening, apologizing, solving the issue, and following up to ensure the customer is satisfied. Use the **L.A.S.T.** method from earlier chapters if applicable.

3. **Apply the plan**: Next time you receive a complaint, follow the plan closely and ensure every step is taken to resolve the issue and rebuild trust.

4. **Follow up**: After resolving the complaint, reach out to the customer again in the following weeks to show you still care about their experience. This extra touch can help transform a negative interaction into a strengthened relationship.

Exercise 7: Rewarding Long-Term Customers

Rewarding long-term customers for their loyalty strengthens your relationship and encourages continued business. This exercise will help you design rewards that resonate with your loyal customers.

Steps:

1. **Identify your most loyal customers**: Analyze your customer data to find those who have been with your business for a long time or frequently return for repeat purchases.

2. **Design a reward program**: Create a reward program specifically for long-term customers. This could include exclusive discounts, early access to new products, or personalized offers that show your appreciation for their loyalty.

3. **Implement the rewards**: Reach out to your long-term customers and let them know they've been selected for

special recognition. Communicate clearly what they'll receive and how their loyalty benefits them.

4. **Track customer reactions**: Monitor how customers respond to the rewards and whether it improves their satisfaction and loyalty to your brand.

Chapter 5: Building Long-Term Relationships with Customers

Chapter 6: Handling Customer Growth and Scaling Your Service

As your business grows, so does your customer base. Growth is a positive sign of success, but it also brings challenges, especially when it comes to maintaining the high standards of customer service that your business was built on. In the early days, it's easier to provide personalized, one-on-one service because your customer base is smaller and you're more directly involved. But as your business expands, scaling your service to meet the needs of a larger audience while retaining that personal touch can become a real challenge.

In this chapter, we'll explore the strategies and systems you can use to scale your customer service without compromising on the **Service First** philosophy that sets your business apart.

Growing Pains: Common Challenges When Scaling Customer Service

When a business starts to grow, it's easy to lose some of the personal attention that early customers loved. The more customers you serve, the more difficult it becomes to manage every interaction personally. If not handled properly, this growth can lead to longer response times, decreased customer satisfaction, and an overall decline in the quality of service.

Here are some common challenges businesses face when scaling customer service:

Chapter 6: Handling Customer Growth and Scaling Your Service

1. **Increased Customer Volume**
   As your customer base grows, so do the number of inquiries, complaints, and support requests. Without the right systems in place, it's easy for your team to become overwhelmed and for customer service to slow down.

2. **Maintaining Personalization**
   With more customers, it becomes harder to keep track of individual preferences, purchase history, and specific needs. This can lead to more generic interactions, which diminishes the personal touch that keeps customers loyal.

3. **Inconsistent Service Levels**
   As your team grows, maintaining consistent service standards can be a challenge. Different employees may handle situations differently, leading to inconsistency in how customers are treated.

4. **Employee Burnout**
   With increased demand comes the risk of overburdening your customer service team. If they're handling too many requests without the right support, it can lead to burnout, decreased morale, and poor customer service.

Maintaining Service Quality as You Grow

Scaling your service without sacrificing quality requires a combination of strategy, training, and technology. The goal is to ensure that even as you grow, your customers still feel valued and receive the same level of attention and care.

1. Documenting and Standardizing Processes

One of the first steps to scaling your service is to document and standardize your processes. This ensures that every customer receives consistent service, no matter who they're interacting with.

- **Creating a Customer Service Playbook**: A customer service playbook outlines your company's policies, procedures, and best practices for handling common customer interactions. It ensures that all team members are on the same page and have clear guidelines for how to respond to different situations.

- **Standardizing Responses**: For frequently asked questions or common issues, create standardized responses that can be used across your team. This not only speeds up response times but also ensures consistency in the information provided to customers.

- **Creating Service Level Agreements (SLAs)**: Set clear expectations for response times and issue resolution. Whether you commit to responding to emails within 24 hours or resolving support tickets within 48 hours, SLAs provide both your team and your customers with clear guidelines on what to expect.

2. Hiring and Training the Right People

As your business grows, so will your customer service team. Hiring the right people and providing them with the proper training is crucial to maintaining the **Service First** standard.

- **Hiring for Empathy and Problem-Solving Skills**: Customer service is more than just answering questions—it's about listening, understanding, and solving problems. When hiring new team members,

Chapter 6: Handling Customer Growth and Scaling Your Service

prioritize empathy and communication skills, as well as the ability to think critically and resolve issues.

- **Providing Continuous Training**: Regularly train your team on customer service best practices, new products or services, and how to handle difficult situations. Continuous training helps ensure that your team is always improving and delivering the best possible service.

- **Empowering Employees**: Encourage your employees to take ownership of customer issues and provide them with the authority to make decisions. Empowered employees can solve problems more quickly and effectively, which leads to a better customer experience.

3. Leveraging Technology to Streamline Service

Technology can be a powerful tool for scaling your customer service without losing the personal touch. The key is to use technology to streamline repetitive tasks while maintaining the ability to provide personalized interactions when needed.

- **Customer Relationship Management (CRM) Systems**: A CRM system helps you manage customer interactions, track preferences, and keep a record of past issues. With a CRM, you can easily access customer information and provide more personalized service, even as your customer base grows.

- **Help Desk and Ticketing Systems**: A ticketing system allows you to organize and prioritize customer inquiries, ensuring that no request falls through the cracks. It also enables your team to collaborate on resolving complex issues and keeps track of response times and resolutions.

- **Live Chat and Chatbots**: Live chat provides customers with real-time support, while chatbots can handle basic inquiries and free up your team to focus on more complex issues. Using chatbots for simple tasks like answering FAQs or providing order updates can help scale your service without sacrificing quality.

4. Automating Where It Makes Sense

Automation can help you scale without compromising on service, but it needs to be used wisely. The goal is to automate repetitive tasks while maintaining the ability to offer personalized service when necessary.

- **Automating Routine Tasks**: Use automation for routine tasks like order confirmations, shipping notifications, and follow-up emails. This frees up your team to focus on more complex customer interactions.

- **Personalizing Automated Interactions**: Even automated interactions can feel personal. For example, use customer data to send personalized follow-up emails or recommendations based on their purchase history. Automation doesn't have to feel robotic — when done right, it can enhance the customer experience.

5. Building a Self-Service Platform

As your business grows, offering self-service options can help reduce the volume of customer inquiries while still providing valuable support. Many customers prefer to find answers on their own, so creating a robust self-service platform is a win-win.

- **Creating a Knowledge Base**: A well-organized knowledge base or FAQ section allows customers to find answers to common questions without needing to contact support. Make sure the information is easy to navigate and regularly updated.

- **Offering Tutorials and How-To Guides**: Provide customers with detailed tutorials, videos, or guides that help them get the most out of your products or services. This not only empowers your customers but also reduces the number of support requests.

Keeping the Personal Touch as You Scale

While technology and automation are crucial for scaling your service, the human element is what makes the **Service First** approach stand out. As you grow, it's important to find ways to maintain the personal touch that keeps customers loyal.

1. Segmenting Your Customer Base
Not all customers require the same level of attention, and segmenting your customer base allows you to tailor your service accordingly. High-value or long-term customers may require more personalized service, while new customers may benefit from more educational resources.

- **VIP Programs**: For your most loyal customers, consider offering a VIP program that provides dedicated support, exclusive offers, or priority service. This makes them feel valued and helps you maintain a strong relationship.

2. Personalized Communication at Scale
Even as your customer base grows, you can still provide personalized communication through thoughtful use of data.

- **Using Customer Data to Personalize Emails**: With the help of CRM systems, you can send personalized emails based on customer behavior, preferences, and purchase history. This makes your communication feel more relevant and meaningful, even at scale.

3. Staying Engaged with Customers

As your business grows, it's easy to lose direct contact with your customers. However, staying engaged and listening to your customers is critical to maintaining the **Service First** standard.

- **Gathering Feedback**: Regularly ask your customers for feedback on their experience. Whether through surveys, reviews, or direct outreach, customer feedback is invaluable for identifying areas for improvement and ensuring that your service remains top-notch as you grow.

- **Monitoring Customer Satisfaction**: Use tools like Net Promoter Scores (NPS) or customer satisfaction surveys to track how well you're meeting customer expectations. This allows you to spot potential issues early and address them before they affect customer loyalty.

Summary

Scaling your customer service as your business grows can be challenging, but with the right strategies in place, you can maintain the same high level of service that earned you your loyal customers in the first place. By standardizing processes, leveraging technology, hiring and training the right people, and automating wisely, you can handle increased customer volume without sacrificing personalization or quality.

Growth doesn't have to mean losing the personal touch that sets your business apart. With a **Service First** mindset, you can scale your operations while ensuring that every customer continues to feel valued and appreciated.

Exercises

Exercise 1: Assessing Your Current Capacity for Growth

This exercise helps you understand your current service capacity and identify areas that may need adjustment as your customer base grows.

Steps:

1. **Review your current service capacity**: Assess your current ability to handle customer inquiries, orders, or support. Consider areas like staffing, response times, and product availability.

2. **Identify bottlenecks**: Look for any parts of your process that are already strained or could become bottlenecks as you scale. For example, do response times increase when demand spikes? Is your inventory system able to handle larger order volumes?

3. **Create an improvement plan**: Develop a plan to address these bottlenecks, such as hiring more staff, automating parts of your process, or improving your inventory management system.

4. **Test scalability**: Simulate a growth scenario by increasing customer volume (e.g., running a promotion or launching a new product). Track how your system responds and adjust the plan based on real-world results.

Exercise 2: Automating Repetitive Tasks

As your customer base grows, automation can help streamline repetitive tasks, saving time and improving efficiency. This exercise helps you identify tasks that can be automated.

Steps:

1. **List repetitive tasks**: Make a list of routine tasks your team regularly performs, such as responding to common customer inquiries, sending follow-up emails, or processing orders.

2. **Identify tasks for automation**: Choose 1-2 tasks from the list that are good candidates for automation. For example, use chatbots to answer frequently asked questions or set up an automated email sequence for customer follow-ups.

3. **Implement automation**: Use a tool or software to automate the selected tasks (e.g., customer relationship management (CRM) tools, email automation platforms, or AI-powered chatbots).

4. **Monitor the impact**: After implementing automation, track how it affects efficiency and customer satisfaction. Does it free up time for your team to focus on more complex tasks while still maintaining a high level of service?

Exercise 3: Scaling Customer Support

As your customer base grows, your support team needs to scale effectively. This exercise helps you build a scalable support system.

Chapter 6: Handling Customer Growth and Scaling Your Service

Steps:

1. **Evaluate your current support system**: Review your current customer support channels (e.g., phone, email, live chat) and identify which ones are most effective. Consider response times, volume of inquiries, and customer satisfaction.

2. **Develop a plan for scaling**: Decide how you will scale your support system to accommodate growth. This could include hiring more staff, outsourcing some support functions, or offering self-service options (e.g., knowledge bases or FAQs).

3. **Test the system**: Introduce a higher volume of support inquiries (e.g., through a promotion or marketing campaign) and observe how your support system handles the load.

4. **Optimize and refine**: Based on the test results, refine your support system to handle more volume without sacrificing quality. Adjust staffing, tools, or processes as needed.

Exercise 4: Maintaining Service Quality During Growth

As your business scales, maintaining service quality becomes more challenging. This exercise helps you ensure that growth doesn't come at the expense of quality.

Steps:

1. **Identify core service standards**: Define the key service standards you want to maintain as you grow, such as response times, product quality, and customer satisfaction.

2. **Assess potential weak points**: Look for areas where growth might threaten service quality. For example, will response times increase as customer inquiries rise? Will product quality suffer if demand outpaces supply?

3. **Develop a plan for maintaining quality**: Create a plan to preserve quality as you grow, such as hiring additional staff, increasing inventory, or implementing more rigorous quality control measures.

4. **Monitor customer feedback**: As your business grows, consistently gather and analyze customer feedback to ensure that service quality remains high. If customers start reporting issues, adjust your strategy to address them quickly.

Exercise 5: Hiring and Training for Growth

Growing customer demand often requires growing your team. This exercise focuses on scaling your workforce while maintaining service quality.

Steps:

1. **Evaluate current staffing levels**: Assess whether your current team can handle projected growth. Look at metrics such as workload, customer interactions, and feedback to identify areas where additional staff may be needed.

2. **Create a hiring plan**: Based on your evaluation, determine which areas need more staff and develop a hiring plan. Consider whether you need full-time employees, part-time help, or external contractors to meet demand.

3. **Develop a training program**: As you onboard new team members, ensure they are properly trained in your company's service standards, culture, and processes. Develop a structured training program that aligns with the **Service First** mindset.

4. **Monitor new hire performance**: Track the performance of new hires to ensure they are meeting the service standards expected of them. Regularly provide feedback and offer additional training where necessary.

Exercise 6: Managing Customer Expectations During Growth

As you scale, it's important to manage customer expectations to avoid disappointment or frustration. This exercise helps you communicate effectively with customers as your business grows.

Steps:

1. **Review current communications**: Analyze the messaging you use with customers in terms of delivery times, service availability, and product availability. Are these realistic as your business grows?

2. **Adjust your messaging**: If needed, adjust your messaging to set more realistic expectations. For example, if longer lead times are expected due to higher demand, communicate this upfront to avoid frustrating customers.

3. **Create proactive updates**: Develop a system for proactively updating customers if there are changes or delays. For example, send regular email updates during busy periods to keep customers informed about their order status.

4. **Track customer satisfaction**: Monitor how well customers respond to the updated communication strategy. Are they more understanding of delays or changes because expectations were set upfront?

Exercise 7: Managing Customer Feedback at Scale

As your customer base grows, handling feedback and incorporating it into your operations becomes more complex. This exercise helps you create a scalable feedback management system.

Steps:

1. **Review your current feedback process**: Assess how you currently gather, analyze, and act on customer feedback. Identify areas that could become overwhelmed as feedback volume increases (e.g., response times to surveys, managing online reviews).

2. **Develop a scalable feedback system**: Implement tools and processes that allow you to handle feedback at scale. This could involve using automated surveys, sentiment analysis tools, or a centralized feedback management platform.

3. **Assign responsibility**: As you scale, assign specific team members or departments to handle feedback in different areas (e.g., product reviews, support feedback, and general customer satisfaction).

4. **Track the impact**: Regularly review customer feedback to identify trends and areas for improvement. Ensure that even as you grow, customer feedback is still valued and acted upon.

Chapter 6: Handling Customer Growth and Scaling Your Service

Chapter 7: Technology and Customer Service

Technology has transformed nearly every aspect of business operations, and customer service is no exception. From live chat to customer relationship management (CRM) systems, technology enables businesses to interact with customers more efficiently, track interactions, and provide better service at scale. However, technology should never replace genuine human interaction—it should complement it. In a **Service First** business, the challenge is to leverage technology to enhance customer service while maintaining a personal, human-centered approach.

This chapter explores how technology can improve your customer service, how to balance digital tools with personal interaction, and which tools can help you deliver a seamless, modern customer experience.

The Role of Technology in Modern Customer Service

Technology has brought significant improvements to customer service, particularly when it comes to speed, convenience, and efficiency. But it's essential to remember that while technology can streamline processes, it's not a replacement for the personal connection that great service requires.

Chapter 7: Technology and Customer Service

Why Technology Matters for Service

Technology allows businesses to scale service, respond to customers faster, and provide more convenience. For example:

- **Instant Communication**: Tools like live chat and chatbots allow customers to get immediate answers to their questions without waiting on hold or sending an email.

- **Personalization**: Customer data stored in CRMs or gathered through online interactions enables businesses to personalize customer interactions, providing more relevant recommendations and support.

- **Self-Service Options**: Many customers prefer to find answers on their own. Online knowledge bases, FAQ sections, and automated systems make it easy for customers to resolve issues without contacting support.

The key to using technology effectively in a **Service First** business is to understand its strengths and limitations. Technology should enhance the customer experience without replacing the personal, human touch that makes customers feel valued.

Leveraging Technology to Improve Service

Here are some of the key ways you can use technology to improve your customer service:

1. CRM Systems

A CRM (Customer Relationship Management) system helps you keep track of customer interactions, preferences, and history. It's an invaluable tool for providing personalized service, as it allows your team to quickly access customer information and offer relevant solutions.

- **Centralizing Customer Data**: A CRM centralizes all customer information—such as contact details, purchase history, and previous interactions—so your team can provide faster and more informed support.

- **Personalizing Interactions**: With customer data at your fingertips, you can personalize interactions by referencing past purchases, preferences, or previous issues. This makes customers feel like you remember and value their business.

- **Tracking Issues**: CRMs help track ongoing support issues, ensuring that nothing falls through the cracks. Your team can see the status of each issue, who's handling it, and when it was last updated, which prevents delays and miscommunication.

2. Live Chat and Chatbots

Live chat allows customers to get instant support, while chatbots can handle routine inquiries, freeing up your team to focus on more complex issues. These tools provide real-time responses and can significantly enhance the customer experience by reducing wait times. However, it's important to use chatbots appropriately. Some customers prefer not to interact with bots and would rather speak to a human. Ensure there is a clear and easy way for customers to escalate to human support when needed. Additionally, you may want to consider using chatbots primarily when your office is closed to cover basic inquiries during off-hours.

- **24/7 Availability**: Chatbots can be available around the clock to answer common questions, assist with orders, or provide basic troubleshooting. This ensures that customers can get help even outside of business hours, improving accessibility and convenience.

- **Escalating to Human Support**: While chatbots are useful for handling basic queries, they should always have an option to escalate to a live agent for more complex issues. This ensures that customers receive the personal attention they need when technology can't fully resolve their problem.

3. Self-Service Platforms

Self-service platforms empower customers to solve their own problems without needing to contact customer support. These platforms can include FAQ sections, knowledge bases, or tutorial videos that guide customers through common issues or questions.

- **Knowledge Base**: A well-organized knowledge base gives customers easy access to information about your products or services. By providing clear, step-by-step guides, you enable customers to troubleshoot on their own, which saves time for both the customer and your support team.

- **Community Forums**: Community forums allow customers to ask questions and share solutions with each other. Not only does this foster a sense of community, but it also reduces the workload for your support team.

4. Automation

Automation can help streamline customer service by handling routine tasks and providing faster responses. However, automation must be used wisely to avoid making customers feel like they're dealing with a robot.

- **Automated Emails**: Use automation to send follow-up emails after purchases, confirm appointments, or notify customers of updates. These communications can feel personal if they're timed correctly and tailored based on customer data.

- **Ticketing Systems**: Automating the process of assigning customer support tickets ensures that each request is handled by the right team member in a timely manner.

5. Data Analytics for Predictive Service

Data analytics can help you anticipate customer needs and improve service before a problem even arises. By analyzing customer behavior, you can identify patterns and trends that signal when a customer might need help, enabling you to take proactive steps.

- **Predictive Support**: Analytics can help you predict when customers might experience an issue based on past behavior or usage data. For example, if you notice that a customer's product is approaching its warranty expiration, you can proactively offer a service plan or replacement options.

- **Customer Feedback Analytics**: Analyzing customer feedback—whether through surveys, reviews, or support interactions—helps identify common pain points. This data allows you to make informed decisions about how to improve your products, services, or support processes.

Chapter 7: Technology and Customer Service

Balancing Technology with the Human Touch

While technology can significantly improve customer service, it's important to maintain a balance between automation and human interaction. Technology should never replace the personal connection that makes customers feel valued.

When to Automate and When to Stay Personal

- **Automate Routine Tasks**: Use technology to handle routine tasks that don't require a personal touch, such as sending order confirmations, processing returns, or answering FAQs.

- **Stay Personal with Complex Issues**: For more complex issues or high-touch interactions, a human response is essential. Customers dealing with problems or confusion often need empathy and reassurance—something a chatbot can't provide.

Maintaining Empathy in Digital Interactions

Even when interacting with customers through digital tools, it's important to maintain empathy. Whether through live chat, email, or social media, your tone and approach should always reflect the same level of care and attention as a face-to-face interaction.

- **Use Personalized Responses**: Avoid using canned responses or generic messages when dealing with customer issues. Instead, personalize your responses based on the specific situation, addressing the customer's concerns directly.

- **Show Understanding**: Customers want to feel heard, even in digital interactions. Use phrases like "I understand how frustrating that must be" or "Let me help you with that" to show empathy and build rapport.

The Future of Technology and Customer Service

Technology is continually evolving, and businesses that embrace new tools and innovations can stay ahead of the curve. Here are some emerging trends that will shape the future of customer service:

1. Artificial Intelligence (AI) and Machine Learning
AI and machine learning are already making an impact on customer service by enabling more advanced chatbots, predictive analytics, and personalized recommendations. As these technologies continue to evolve, businesses will be able to provide even more tailored and efficient service.

- **AI-Powered Chatbots**: AI-powered chatbots can handle more complex interactions, learning from previous conversations to provide more accurate and helpful responses.

- **Predictive Personalization**: Machine learning algorithms can analyze customer behavior to predict their needs and provide personalized solutions before they even ask.

2. Voice Assistants

As voice technology continues to grow, more businesses are integrating voice assistants into their customer service platforms. Customers can use voice commands to get information, place orders, or troubleshoot issues without needing to type or navigate a website.

- **Voice-Activated Support**: Customers can use voice assistants like Alexa, Google Assistant, or Siri to interact with your business, making the support process faster and more convenient.

3. Augmented Reality (AR) and Virtual Reality (VR)

AR and VR are opening up new possibilities for customer service, especially in industries like retail, real estate, and technology. These technologies allow customers to virtually try products, explore spaces, or receive hands-on troubleshooting support.

- **Virtual Product Demos**: Using AR or VR, customers can experience products in a virtual environment before making a purchase, reducing uncertainty and improving satisfaction.

- **Immersive Support**: AR can be used to guide customers through complex troubleshooting processes by overlaying instructions onto their real-world environment.

Summary

Technology has revolutionized customer service, making it faster, more efficient, and more convenient for both businesses and customers. From CRMs and live chat to AI-powered chatbots and predictive analytics, the right tools can help you provide better service at scale. However, in a **Service First** business, technology should always support — not replace — genuine human interaction.

The key is to find the right balance between automation and personal service, using technology to streamline processes while ensuring that customers still receive the empathy and care they deserve. By leveraging the right tools and staying ahead of emerging trends, you can deliver a seamless, modern customer experience that keeps customers coming back.

Exercises

Exercise 1: Evaluating Your Current Technology

This exercise helps you assess the effectiveness of the current technology tools you're using in your customer service operations.

Steps:

1. **List the technology tools you currently use**: Identify the tools you use for customer service, such as live chat, chatbots, CRM systems, helpdesk software, or automated email responses.

2. **Evaluate their effectiveness**: For each tool, evaluate how well it serves its purpose. Does it improve efficiency? How do customers respond to it? Are there any frequent issues or complaints?

3. **Identify gaps**: Look for areas where your current technology might be falling short. For example, are there too many customer inquiries that chatbots can't handle? Are there delays in ticket responses?

4. **Create an action plan**: Based on your evaluation, create a plan to address gaps. This might include upgrading your CRM, improving chatbot functionality, or offering more ways for customers to reach human support.

Exercise 2: Balancing Automation with Human Interaction

This exercise helps you find the right balance between using automated systems and maintaining human interaction for customer service.

Steps:

1. **Identify automated processes**: Make a list of tasks currently handled by automation in your customer service (e.g., automated email responses, chatbot interactions, or ticketing systems).

2. **Review customer feedback**: Look at recent customer feedback or survey responses to see how customers feel about the automation. Do they prefer more human interaction in certain areas?

3. **Determine points of escalation**: Identify points where customers may need to be escalated to a human for more personalized assistance. For example, complex issues or questions that fall outside of standard queries.

4. **Create an escalation protocol**: Develop a clear process for when and how customers can transition from automation to human support. Ensure that chatbots and

automated systems make it easy for customers to request human assistance.

Exercise 3: Enhancing 24/7 Availability with Chatbots

This exercise focuses on implementing or improving chatbot systems to provide round-the-clock support.

Steps:

1. **Identify common customer queries**: Look at frequent questions or issues your customers have (e.g., order status, troubleshooting, product availability). These are prime candidates for chatbot automation.

2. **Develop chatbot scripts**: Write out responses that a chatbot could use to address these common questions. Ensure the language is clear, friendly, and helpful.

3. **Test the chatbot**: Set up your chatbot to handle these queries and run tests to see how well it responds to customer inquiries. Simulate different scenarios to ensure the chatbot performs effectively.

4. **Monitor usage and feedback**: Once the chatbot is live, track its performance and gather customer feedback. Are customers satisfied with the responses? Are they able to transition easily to human support if needed?

Exercise 4: Improving the Use of CRM Systems

Customer Relationship Management (CRM) systems can help you track interactions and improve personalized service. This exercise helps you optimize your CRM use.

Steps:

1. **Review your CRM data**: Analyze how your CRM system is currently being used. Are customer interactions, preferences, and histories being logged accurately and consistently?

2. **Identify areas for improvement**: Look for gaps in how your CRM is used. Are follow-up reminders being utilized? Is customer data being used to personalize interactions?

3. **Optimize CRM workflows**: Set up automated workflows within your CRM to streamline tasks like follow-ups, birthday messages, or feedback requests. Ensure that your team is using these workflows consistently.

4. **Train your team**: Provide additional training for your team to ensure they are using the CRM to its full potential. This could include tracking customer preferences, creating detailed records, or using data for more personalized communication.

Exercise 5: Using Technology for Proactive Customer Support

Proactive customer service can reduce the number of incoming support requests by addressing issues before they arise. This exercise helps you use technology to anticipate customer needs.

Steps:

1. **Identify recurring issues**: Look through your support data to find common issues that customers face (e.g., confusion with a product feature, delivery delays).

2. **Create proactive communication**: Develop automated email or SMS messages that address these issues before

customers need to reach out. For example, send a troubleshooting guide right after a purchase, or an update if there's a known delay in shipping.

3. **Set up automated triggers**: Use your CRM or email system to send these proactive messages based on customer actions (e.g., after a purchase, when an issue is detected, or during high-traffic periods).

4. **Monitor effectiveness**: Track whether the proactive messages reduce the number of support requests and whether customers respond positively to the additional help.

Exercise 6: Personalizing Service with Technology

Technology can be used to offer personalized service, which improves customer satisfaction. This exercise helps you implement more personalized experiences using the tools you have.

Steps:

1. **Analyze customer data**: Use your CRM or customer database to review what data you collect about customers, such as purchase history, preferences, or past interactions.

2. **Identify personalization opportunities**: Think about ways you could personalize interactions. For example, send recommendations based on past purchases, offer discounts for products they frequently buy, or send personalized thank-you messages.

3. **Set up automation for personalization**: Implement personalized emails or messages based on customer

behavior. For example, if a customer hasn't purchased in a while, send them a personalized re-engagement message with a special offer.

4. **Measure customer response**: Track how customers respond to personalized communication. Are they more likely to engage with your business when they receive personalized offers or messages?

Exercise 7: Managing Multiple Channels with Technology

Handling customer inquiries across multiple channels (email, phone, chat, social media) can be overwhelming without proper systems in place. This exercise helps you streamline multi-channel support.

Steps:

1. **List all communication channels**: Identify every channel through which customers can contact your business, such as social media, live chat, email, phone, or support tickets.

2. **Evaluate response times**: For each channel, evaluate how quickly and effectively your team responds. Are some channels being neglected? Are others overburdened?

3. **Implement multi-channel management tools**: If you're not already using one, consider implementing a tool that integrates multiple channels into one platform (e.g., a helpdesk tool or unified inbox).

4. **Monitor customer satisfaction**: After streamlining your multi-channel approach, track whether customers are receiving faster and more consistent responses across all channels.

Chapter 7: Technology and Customer Service

Chapter 8: Leading by Example

In any organization, the culture around customer service is shaped from the top down. As a business owner or leader, your attitude toward customer service, the standards you set, and the way you interact with customers serve as the blueprint for your team's behavior. When you prioritize customer service and demonstrate a **Service First** mentality, your team is more likely to follow suit. In contrast, if customer service isn't a focus for leadership, it's unlikely to be a priority for your employees.

This chapter explores the importance of leading by example, how to model the customer service behaviors you want to see in your team, and when to step in as a business owner during tough situations.

Setting the Standard for Customer Service

As a business owner, you set the tone for customer service within your organization. Your team will look to you for cues on how to handle customers, resolve issues, and balance competing priorities. Leading by example means embodying the values of **Service First** in every interaction, whether it's with your employees or directly with customers.

Why Leadership Matters

Employees take their cues from leadership. If they see you treating customers with respect, going above and beyond to solve problems, and valuing customer feedback, they will be more likely to do the same. Your actions set the bar for what's acceptable and expected in customer service.

- **Building a Customer-Centric Culture**: A **Service First** business is built on a customer-centric culture, and that starts with leadership. When you, as the leader, prioritize customer satisfaction, it becomes a core part of your company's identity.

- **Reinforcing Expectations**: By consistently demonstrating excellent customer service, you reinforce your expectations for the rest of the team. This doesn't just apply to front-line employees — every department, from marketing to finance, plays a role in delivering great service.

Walking the Talk

It's easy to talk about the importance of customer service, but it's your actions that will resonate with your team. "Walking the talk" means actively demonstrating the behaviors you want your employees to embody.

- **Handling Customer Interactions**: Whenever possible, interact directly with customers to show your team how it's done. Whether it's responding to a customer's email, handling a complaint, or checking in after a sale, your involvement demonstrates that no customer is too small or issue too insignificant for leadership to address.

- **Showing Empathy and Respect**: As a leader, show empathy and respect in every interaction, both with customers and employees. How you treat others sets the tone for how your employees will treat customers. Leading with empathy not only fosters better relationships with your team but also models the kind of service mentality you want to see across the organization.

Encouraging a Customer-First Mindset

It's not enough to just model good behavior — you also need to encourage and empower your team to adopt a **Service First** mindset. This involves creating an environment where employees feel valued and motivated to prioritize customer service.

Empowering Employees to Make Decisions

One of the biggest barriers to excellent customer service is rigid policies or a lack of authority among front-line employees. If your team doesn't feel empowered to resolve issues or make decisions in the moment, they'll struggle to deliver the kind of service that keeps customers loyal.

- **Trusting Employees to Take Action**: Encourage your team to take ownership of customer interactions. Let them know that you trust their judgment and empower them to solve problems without needing constant approval. Whether it's offering a refund, providing an alternative solution, or simply listening to a customer's concerns, give your employees the freedom to act in the customer's best interest.

- **Providing the Right Tools and Training**: Empowerment also comes from equipping your team with the right tools and training. Make sure your employees have the resources they need to handle customer requests efficiently, from access to customer data in your CRM system to training on conflict resolution and communication skills.

Recognizing and Rewarding Great Service

Recognition goes a long way in motivating employees to deliver excellent customer service. When you actively recognize and reward employees who go above and beyond for customers, you reinforce the importance of service in your organization's culture.

- **Public Recognition**: Whether in team meetings, company-wide emails, or informal shout-outs, publicly recognizing employees who provide outstanding service boosts morale and encourages others to follow suit.

- **Service Awards or Bonuses**: Consider creating service awards or offering bonuses for employees who consistently receive positive customer feedback or resolve challenging issues. These incentives can help keep customer service top of mind and show your team that their efforts are appreciated.

Stepping In During Tough Situations

While your team will handle most customer interactions, there will be times when you, as the business owner, need to step in. Whether it's a particularly difficult customer, a high-stakes issue, or a complaint that has escalated beyond your team's control, your involvement can make all the difference.

When to Step In

Knowing when to step in as the leader is key to resolving tough situations. While you don't want to micromanage or undermine your team's authority, certain scenarios require your direct attention:

- **High-Profile Clients**: If the issue involves a high-profile or long-term customer, it may be worth your time to personally reach out and ensure the matter is handled with care. Your involvement can help strengthen the relationship and demonstrate your commitment to customer satisfaction.

- **Escalated Complaints**: If a customer complaint has escalated to the point where your team is unable to resolve it, stepping in can help de-escalate the situation. Customers are often reassured when they see that the business owner is personally involved in resolving their issue.

- **Serious Service Failures**: If there's been a significant service failure—such as a major product defect, a delay in a critical delivery, or a data breach—personally addressing the issue can help rebuild trust with the customer. Taking ownership of the situation and offering a solution directly shows accountability and care.

How to Lead in Crisis

When you do step in during tough situations, it's important to handle the interaction with calm, empathy, and transparency. How you navigate these situations sets the standard for how your team will approach future challenges.

- **Stay Calm and Focused**: Customers in crisis may be frustrated or upset, but it's important to remain calm and focused on resolving the issue. Reassure the customer that their concerns are being taken seriously and that you're committed to finding a solution.

- **Be Transparent and Honest**: Customers appreciate honesty, even when the news isn't good. If there's been a mistake or service failure, acknowledge it, apologize sincerely, and explain the steps you're taking to fix it. Transparency builds trust, and customers are more likely to forgive a mistake if they feel you're being open and honest with them.

- **Follow Through on Promises**: If you promise a solution, make sure it happens. Whether it's a refund, a replacement, or a future discount, follow through on your commitments to show customers that you stand by your word.

Building a Culture of Accountability

Leading by example means holding yourself and your team accountable for delivering excellent customer service. Accountability is about taking responsibility for both successes and failures, learning from mistakes, and continuously improving.

Encouraging a Culture of Continuous Improvement

In a **Service First** business, there's always room for improvement. Encourage your team to view feedback — whether positive or negative — as an opportunity to learn and grow.

- **Reviewing Customer Feedback**: Regularly review customer feedback with your team to identify areas where you're excelling and areas where you can improve. Use this feedback to make changes, whether it's improving a process, refining a policy, or adjusting how your team communicates with customers.

- **Learning from Mistakes**: Mistakes are inevitable, but how you handle them is what matters. Encourage your team to take ownership of mistakes and view them as learning opportunities rather than failures. As the leader, model this behavior by acknowledging when something went wrong and showing how to make it right.

Summary

Leading by example is one of the most powerful ways to build a **Service First** culture in your business. When you prioritize customer service in your own actions, your team will follow suit. Empower your employees to take ownership of customer interactions, recognize and reward great service, and step in when necessary to handle tough situations. By setting the standard for customer service and holding yourself and your team accountable, you can create a culture where excellent service is the norm, not the exception.

Chapter 8: Leading by Example

In the next chapter, we'll dive into how to measure and improve your customer service over time, ensuring that your **Service First** approach continues to evolve and adapt to your customers' needs.

Exercises

Exercise 1: Reflecting on Your Leadership Style

Leaders set the tone for customer service within their organization. This exercise helps you reflect on how your actions and behavior influence your team's approach to service.

Steps:

1. **Analyze your leadership style**: Reflect on how you currently lead your team. Do you actively engage with customer service processes? How do you handle customer issues, and how does your approach influence your team?

2. **Identify areas for improvement**: Consider areas where you can improve as a leader in customer service. For example, do you model patience and empathy when dealing with difficult customers? Do you provide support and guidance for your team when they need it?

3. **Set a leadership goal**: Based on your reflection, set a goal for how you will improve your leadership. For example, commit to handling customer complaints with a positive attitude in front of your team or to regularly participate in customer support activities to show your involvement.

4. **Track your progress**: Over the next few weeks, track how your changes in behavior impact your team's approach

to customer service. Are they more engaged, empathetic, or proactive?

Exercise 2: Shadowing Your Team

Leaders can gain valuable insights by observing their team members as they interact with customers. This exercise helps you learn from your team and identify areas where you can provide guidance.

Steps:

1. **Schedule a shadowing session**: Set aside time to shadow one of your customer service team members during their interactions with customers. Pay attention to how they handle inquiries, complaints, and general interactions.

2. **Observe without interrupting**: During the shadowing session, observe the employee's approach without stepping in. Take note of both their strengths and areas where they could improve.

3. **Offer constructive feedback**: After the session, provide constructive feedback. Focus on what the team member did well and offer suggestions for improvement if needed. Emphasize positive behavior that aligns with your company's customer service goals.

4. **Lead by example**: After the shadowing session, handle a few customer inquiries yourself in front of the team. Demonstrate your commitment to high-quality service and show how you address issues with a **Service First** mindset.

Exercise 3: Modeling Empathy in Customer Interactions

Chapter 8: Leading by Example

Empathy is a key trait for leaders in customer service. This exercise helps you practice and model empathetic behavior for your team.

Steps:

1. **Reflect on recent customer interactions**: Think about a recent situation where a customer was frustrated or upset. How did you or your team handle the situation? Was empathy at the forefront of the response?

2. **Role-play an empathetic response**: Choose a common customer service scenario (e.g., a delayed order or a product issue). Role-play with a team member, modeling an empathetic response. Show how you actively listen, acknowledge the customer's frustration, and offer a solution.

3. **Encourage your team to practice empathy**: After modeling an empathetic response, encourage your team to practice the same. Have them role-play handling a difficult customer while focusing on empathy.

4. **Monitor team behavior**: In the following weeks, observe whether your team becomes more empathetic in their customer interactions. Provide additional feedback and support where needed.

Exercise 4: Leading in Difficult Situations

As a leader, you're expected to guide your team through challenging situations. This exercise helps you develop strategies for leading your team during crises or high-pressure moments.

Steps:

1. **Identify a challenging situation**: Reflect on a recent crisis or high-pressure moment your business faced (e.g., a service outage, a large influx of customer complaints). How did you and your team handle the situation?

2. **Assess your leadership during the situation**: Consider how you led during the challenge. Did you remain calm and composed? Did you communicate effectively with your team? Were you involved in problem-solving, or did you leave it to others?

3. **Develop a leadership strategy**: Based on your reflection, develop a strategy for leading during future crises. This could include clear communication protocols, delegating tasks effectively, and ensuring you're visible and available to guide the team.

4. **Simulate a crisis**: Run a simulation with your team to practice handling a difficult situation. Guide your team through the steps, providing support and clear direction. Afterward, debrief with the team and ask for feedback on your leadership.

Exercise 5: Setting a Standard for Customer Service

Leaders set the standard for customer service within their organization. This exercise helps you define the service standards you want your team to follow.

Steps:

1. **Define your customer service standards**: Think about the key values you want to instill in your team (e.g., empathy, responsiveness, thoroughness). Write down specific standards that you believe are essential for delivering exceptional customer service.

2. **Communicate your standards**: Share these standards with your team during a meeting. Explain why they are important and how they will impact customer satisfaction and loyalty.

3. **Demonstrate the standards**: Model these standards in your own customer interactions. For example, if one of your standards is quick response times, demonstrate how you respond to customer inquiries promptly and efficiently.

4. **Monitor adherence**: Over the next few weeks, monitor whether your team is meeting the service standards. Offer praise for team members who consistently follow the standards and provide guidance to those who need improvement.

Exercise 6: Encouraging Accountability in Your Team

Leaders should foster a culture of accountability within their teams. This exercise focuses on promoting responsibility and ownership in customer service.

Steps:

1. **Discuss accountability with your team**: Hold a team meeting to discuss the importance of taking responsibility for both successes and mistakes in customer service. Emphasize how accountability leads to growth and improvement.

2. **Assign ownership of customer interactions**: Encourage team members to take full ownership of customer inquiries from start to finish. For example, when a customer issue arises, the team member handling it

Chapter 8: Leading by Example

should see it through until it's resolved, rather than passing it off to someone else.

3. **Lead by example**: Model accountability in your own actions. If something goes wrong in customer service, take responsibility for your role in the situation and demonstrate how you'll work to correct it.

4. **Acknowledge accountability**: When team members show accountability, acknowledge it publicly. Praise them for taking ownership and finding solutions, reinforcing the value of responsibility.

Exercise 7: Leading with Continuous Improvement

Effective leaders focus on continuous improvement in customer service. This exercise helps you foster a mindset of constant growth within your team.

Steps:

1. **Review recent customer service performance**: Analyze recent customer feedback or service performance metrics. Identify areas where your team is excelling and areas where there is room for improvement.

2. **Set improvement goals**: Based on your analysis, set specific improvement goals for your team (e.g., reducing response times, increasing customer satisfaction scores). Share these goals with the team and explain how achieving them will benefit both customers and the team.

3. **Lead an improvement project**: Choose one area for improvement and lead a project to address it. For example, if response times are slow, work with the team

to streamline processes or introduce new tools to speed things up.

4. **Celebrate progress**: As your team works toward improvement, celebrate milestones and acknowledge their hard work. Encouraging continuous improvement will inspire the team to keep striving for excellence in customer service.

Chapter 9: Measuring and Improving Customer Service

Providing excellent customer service is an ongoing process, and in a **Service First** business, there's always room for improvement. The key to maintaining high standards is to regularly measure the effectiveness of your service efforts, gather feedback, and make data-driven decisions to enhance the customer experience. By identifying what's working well and where improvements can be made, you can ensure that your business continues to meet and exceed customer expectations.

In this chapter, we'll explore how to measure customer service performance using key metrics, how to gather and interpret customer feedback, and practical strategies for continuous improvement.

Why Measuring Customer Service is Important

Customer service can feel intangible—after all, it's largely based on interactions, feelings, and relationships. However, measuring customer service is critical to understanding its impact on your business and identifying areas for improvement.

The Benefits of Measuring Service Performance

- **Understanding Customer Satisfaction**: Measuring customer service helps you understand how satisfied your customers are and what factors contribute to their experience. High satisfaction rates often translate into loyalty, repeat business, and positive word of mouth.

- **Identifying Weaknesses**: No matter how excellent your service is, there will always be areas where you can improve. Tracking service performance helps you identify pain points, inefficiencies, or recurring issues that may be hindering your customers' experience.

- **Tracking Progress Over Time**: Regularly measuring service performance allows you to track progress and improvements over time. It also helps you identify trends, such as seasonal fluctuations in service quality or recurring issues that need to be addressed.

The Key to Data-Driven Improvement

When you have clear data about how your service is performing, you can make informed, data-driven decisions to improve. Instead of guessing what might improve customer satisfaction, you can rely on hard numbers to show what's working and where there's room for growth.

Key Metrics for Measuring Customer Service

There are several key metrics that provide insight into how well your customer service efforts are performing. These metrics, when tracked consistently, can give you a clear picture of the customer experience and highlight areas for improvement.

1. Customer Satisfaction (CSAT)

CSAT is one of the most commonly used metrics to measure customer service. It reflects how satisfied customers are with a specific interaction, product, or service. After a customer interacts with your business — whether they've made a purchase or contacted customer support — you can ask them to rate their satisfaction on a scale (e.g., 1 to 5 or 1 to 10).

- **Why It Matters**: CSAT provides direct feedback on how well your business is meeting customer expectations. A high CSAT score indicates that your service is effective and customers are leaving interactions satisfied.

- **How to Measure It**: You can measure CSAT through post-interaction surveys, feedback forms, or follow-up emails asking customers to rate their experience.

2. Net Promoter Score (NPS)

NPS is a metric that measures customer loyalty by asking customers how likely they are to recommend your business to others. It's a simple, yet powerful way to gauge how your customers feel about your brand as a whole.

- **How It Works**: NPS is typically measured by asking customers, "On a scale of 0 to 10, how likely are you to recommend us to a friend or colleague?" Based on their answers, customers are classified as Promoters (9–10), Passives (7–8), or Detractors (0–6). NPS is calculated by subtracting the percentage of Detractors from the percentage of Promoters.

- **Why It Matters**: NPS provides insight into overall customer loyalty and how your brand is perceived. A high NPS score indicates strong loyalty and that customers are happy enough to recommend your business to others.

Chapter 9: Measuring and Improving Customer Service

3. First Response Time

First response time measures how long it takes for your team to respond to a customer inquiry. Whether it's via email, live chat, or social media, customers expect quick responses, and delays can lead to frustration.

- **Why It Matters**: Fast response times show that your business values customers' time and is committed to resolving issues quickly. Shorter response times are often linked to higher satisfaction rates.

- **How to Measure It**: Track how long it takes from when a customer submits a request to when they receive their first response from your team. This metric can be calculated using your help desk or CRM system.

4. Resolution Time

Resolution time refers to how long it takes for your team to fully resolve a customer issue or inquiry. The faster you can resolve problems, the more satisfied your customers are likely to be.

- **Why It Matters**: While quick responses are important, what truly matters to customers is how quickly their problem is resolved. A short resolution time indicates efficiency and a commitment to solving customer issues promptly.

- **How to Measure It**: Measure the time from when the customer first contacts your team to when their issue is fully resolved. This metric helps identify bottlenecks in your service processes.

5. Customer Retention Rate

Customer retention rate measures the percentage of customers who continue doing business with you over a specific period. It's a key indicator of loyalty and the effectiveness of your customer service.

- **Why It Matters**: Retaining existing customers is often more cost-effective than acquiring new ones. A high retention rate indicates that your customers are happy with your products and services and are less likely to leave for competitors.

- **How to Measure It**: Calculate customer retention by comparing the number of customers at the start of a given period with the number who are still customers at the end of that period.

Gathering and Interpreting Customer Feedback

Customer feedback is one of the most valuable tools for improving your service. Whether it comes from surveys, reviews, or informal conversations, feedback gives you direct insight into what your customers are experiencing and how you can improve.

1. Asking for Feedback

The best way to understand how your customers feel about your service is to ask them directly. There are several ways to gather feedback:

- **Post-Interaction Surveys**: After a customer completes a transaction or contacts customer support, send a short survey asking about their experience. These surveys can be as simple as asking them to rate their satisfaction or include more detailed questions about specific aspects of the interaction.

- **Email Follow-Ups**: Send follow-up emails after key touchpoints (e.g., after a purchase, after support interaction) asking for feedback. Make it easy for customers to respond with a quick rating or comment.

- **Social Media and Reviews**: Pay attention to what customers are saying about your business on social media, review sites, or forums. While this feedback may be unsolicited, it provides valuable insights into how customers perceive your brand.

2. Analyzing Feedback for Actionable Insights

Once you've gathered feedback, it's important to analyze it to uncover trends, identify pain points, and highlight areas for improvement.

- **Look for Common Themes**: As you review feedback, look for patterns or recurring issues. Are multiple customers mentioning the same problem? Are there frequent complaints about response times, product quality, or ease of use? Identifying common themes helps you pinpoint where improvements are needed.

- **Distinguish Between Isolated Issues and Systemic Problems**: Not all negative feedback indicates a systemic issue. Some complaints may be isolated incidents, while others point to broader problems that need to be addressed across your team or processes.

- **Use Both Positive and Negative Feedback**: While it's easy to focus on negative feedback, positive feedback is equally important. Pay attention to what customers like about your service and build on those strengths to further improve their experience.

Strategies for Continuous Improvement

Once you've gathered data and feedback, the next step is to take action. Improving customer service is an ongoing process, and it requires both short-term fixes and long-term strategies to ensure you're continually evolving.

1. Act on Feedback Quickly
When you identify areas for improvement, take action as quickly as possible. Whether it's resolving an issue for an individual customer or making broader changes to your service process, quick action demonstrates that you're committed to improving the customer experience.

- **Immediate Fixes**: If feedback reveals a specific issue (e.g., a problem with product functionality, long wait times for support), address it immediately. Communicate with the customer to let them know you're taking their concerns seriously and explain what steps you're taking to fix the issue.

- **Team-Wide Improvements**: If feedback highlights a recurring problem or process inefficiency, take a broader approach. This could involve revising training materials, updating your customer service playbook, or adjusting your staffing levels to ensure customers are served more efficiently.

2. Set Improvement Goals and Track Progress
Improving customer service requires setting clear goals and tracking your progress over time. Use the metrics you're already tracking—like CSAT, NPS, or resolution time—as benchmarks, and set realistic goals for improvement.

- **Improving Response Times**: For example, if your first response time is longer than you'd like, set a goal to reduce it by 10% over the next quarter. Track your progress and identify specific actions your team can take to meet the goal.

- **Improving Satisfaction Scores**: If your CSAT score is lower than expected, focus on addressing the specific areas where customers are dissatisfied, whether it's product quality, communication, or response times.

3. Foster a Culture of Continuous Improvement

Create a culture within your organization where continuous improvement is valued and encouraged. Make it clear that customer service isn't a static function—it's a process that can always be refined and optimized.

- **Regular Team Reviews**: Schedule regular reviews with your customer service team to discuss feedback, metrics, and areas for improvement. Encourage employees to share their own insights and ideas for improving service.

- **Celebrate Wins**: When you reach improvement goals or receive positive feedback, celebrate those wins with your team. Recognizing successes reinforces the importance of providing great customer service.

Summary

Measuring and improving customer service is essential to maintaining a **Service First** business. By tracking key metrics like customer satisfaction, response times, and retention rates, and gathering meaningful feedback from customers, you can identify areas for improvement and take action to enhance the customer experience. Continuous improvement requires both immediate fixes and long-term strategies, but the result is a more responsive, customer-centric business that consistently meets and exceeds expectations.

In the final chapter, we'll look at real-world examples of businesses that excel at customer service and the lessons you can apply to your own organization.

Exercises

Exercise 1: Defining Key Customer Service Metrics

This exercise helps you identify and define the key metrics that will measure the success of your customer service efforts.

Steps:

1. **Identify key metrics**: List the most important metrics that reflect the health of your customer service. Common metrics include:

    - **Customer Satisfaction (CSAT)**: How satisfied customers are with their interactions.

    - **Net Promoter Score (NPS)**: How likely customers are to recommend your business.

- **First Response Time (FRT)**: How long it takes for customers to receive an initial response.
- **Resolution Time**: The average time it takes to resolve customer issues.

2. **Set benchmarks**: Establish benchmarks for each metric based on your industry standards or previous performance. For example, if your average response time is 2 hours, aim to reduce it to 1 hour.

3. **Track metrics over time**: Set up a system to track these metrics consistently (e.g., through customer surveys, CRM software, or analytics tools).

4. **Review and adjust**: Review the data after a set period (e.g., monthly or quarterly) and adjust your processes if certain metrics aren't meeting your benchmarks.

Exercise 2: Gathering Customer Feedback

Customer feedback is essential for measuring service quality. This exercise focuses on collecting and analyzing feedback from your customers.

Steps:

1. **Choose feedback channels**: Decide how you'll collect customer feedback. Options include post-interaction surveys, email surveys, online reviews, or social media monitoring.

2. **Create a simple survey**: Design a short survey with a mix of quantitative and qualitative questions. Include:
   - Rating scales (e.g., "How satisfied were you with your service experience on a scale of 1-10?")

- Open-ended questions (e.g., "What could we have done better?")

3. **Send the survey**: After each customer interaction, send a follow-up survey asking for feedback. Automate this process to ensure consistency.

4. **Analyze the results**: Review the feedback to identify common themes. Are customers consistently satisfied, or are there recurring issues? Use this information to pinpoint areas for improvement.

Exercise 3: Improving First Response and Resolution Times

This exercise focuses on reducing the time it takes to respond to and resolve customer issues, which directly impacts customer satisfaction.

Steps:

1. **Track current response and resolution times**: Use your customer service software to measure how long it currently takes your team to respond to and resolve customer inquiries.

2. **Identify bottlenecks**: Look for areas where response or resolution times are slowed down. For example, are certain types of inquiries taking longer to resolve? Are there delays in communication between teams?

3. **Set a target for improvement**: Based on your current metrics, set specific goals to improve both response and resolution times (e.g., reducing first response time from 2 hours to 1 hour).

4. **Implement changes**: Take steps to meet your goals, such as adjusting team workflows, automating common inquiries, or hiring more staff if needed.

5. **Monitor progress**: Track your metrics over time to see if the changes improve response and resolution times. Adjust your strategy as necessary.

Exercise 4: Analyzing Customer Complaints

This exercise helps you turn customer complaints into opportunities for improvement.

Steps:

1. **Collect recent complaints**: Gather a sample of recent customer complaints or negative feedback from multiple channels (e.g., support tickets, online reviews, or emails).

2. **Categorize the complaints**: Group the complaints into categories based on common themes (e.g., product issues, shipping delays, customer support quality).

3. **Identify root causes**: For each category, identify the root cause of the complaints. Are they caused by unclear communication, internal process failures, or technical issues?

4. **Create an action plan**: Develop a plan to address the root causes. For example, if shipping delays are common, look into improving your logistics process, or if support quality is a frequent issue, provide additional training for your team.

5. **Track resolution**: After implementing changes, continue monitoring customer feedback to see if the number of complaints in each category decreases.

Exercise 5: Conducting Customer Service Audits

Customer service audits provide a comprehensive view of how well your service processes are performing. This exercise will help you conduct an internal audit.

Steps:

1. **Audit communication channels**: Evaluate each communication channel (e.g., phone, email, chat) to ensure they are working efficiently. For example, check whether response times differ between channels and whether customer inquiries are being handled consistently across them.

2. **Audit service processes**: Review your processes for handling customer inquiries, escalations, and resolutions. Are there clear guidelines for each step of the customer journey? Is your team following them consistently?

3. **Evaluate customer feedback**: Look at customer feedback to identify areas where service is strong and where it needs improvement. Use metrics like CSAT and NPS scores to measure overall satisfaction.

4. **Implement improvements**: Based on your audit findings, implement changes to streamline service processes or improve communication. For example, if live chat response times are slow, consider adding more staff during peak hours.

5. **Repeat regularly**: Conduct audits on a regular basis (e.g., quarterly or annually) to ensure that your customer service processes continue to improve over time.

Chapter 9: Measuring and Improving Customer Service

Exercise 6: Benchmarking Against Industry Standards

This exercise helps you compare your customer service performance to industry standards to identify areas where you can improve.

Steps:

1. **Research industry benchmarks**: Research customer service benchmarks for your industry. This could include metrics like average response times, NPS scores, or customer satisfaction levels.

2. **Compare your performance**: Compare your own metrics (e.g., CSAT, NPS, response times) against these benchmarks. Are you exceeding industry standards, or are there areas where you fall short?

3. **Set improvement goals**: Based on the comparison, set specific goals to either match or exceed industry standards. For example, if your industry's average response time is 2 hours and yours is 3, aim to reduce your response time to meet the industry average or beat it.

4. **Implement strategies**: Take steps to achieve your improvement goals, such as using automation to speed up responses or offering more personalized service to increase customer satisfaction.

5. **Track your progress**: Monitor your metrics regularly to ensure that your performance is improving and that you're staying ahead of or on par with industry benchmarks.

Exercise 7: Fostering a Culture of Continuous Improvement

This exercise encourages you to create a culture where your team is constantly seeking ways to improve customer service.

Steps:

1. **Hold team discussions**: Regularly hold team meetings or discussions focused on improving customer service. Encourage team members to share their thoughts on what's working and what can be improved.

2. **Gather improvement ideas**: Ask your team for ideas on how to improve customer service processes. Are there tools or technologies that could help? Do they see recurring issues that need to be addressed?

3. **Implement a suggestion system**: Create a formal system where team members can submit suggestions for improving customer service. Reward or recognize those whose suggestions lead to measurable improvements.

4. **Track and celebrate improvements**: Track the impact of any changes that come from team suggestions. Celebrate successes and use them as motivation for continuous improvement.

Chapter 9: Measuring and Improving Customer Service

Chapter 10: Case Studies and Real-World Examples

The best way to understand the power of great customer service is to see it in action. Throughout this book, we've discussed the principles and strategies that form the foundation of a **Service First** business, but how do those principles play out in the real world? In this chapter, we'll explore real-world examples of businesses that have built lasting success through exceptional customer service. These case studies illustrate the impact of a customer-first approach, from small companies to global brands.

Whether it's turning a negative experience into a positive one or going above and beyond to create customer loyalty, these examples show how customer service can drive business growth, enhance reputation, and create deep, lasting connections with customers.

Case Study 1: Zappos – Building Loyalty Through Extraordinary Service

Zappos, an online shoe and clothing retailer, is known worldwide for its commitment to customer service. From the beginning, Zappos built its brand around one simple idea: provide extraordinary customer service, no matter the cost. What sets Zappos apart is their willingness to go above and beyond for customers, even if it means operating at a loss on individual transactions.

Chapter 10: Case Studies and Real-World Examples

Key Takeaways:

- **Service Above Sales**: Zappos encourages its employees to focus on service, not sales. There's no pressure to upsell or rush through calls, which fosters genuine, long-lasting relationships with customers.

- **Customer-Focused Policies**: Zappos offers a 365-day return policy, free shipping, and even free return shipping, removing barriers that might make customers hesitant to buy online. This level of generosity not only reassures customers but also builds trust and loyalty.

- **Empowering Employees**: Zappos empowers its customer service representatives to take as much time as needed to help each customer. There are no strict call limits, and employees have the autonomy to resolve issues as they see fit, even if it means sending a free replacement or upgrading shipping.

Lesson: When you prioritize customer service over short-term profit, you create loyalty that pays off in the long run. Zappos' commitment to providing exceptional service, no matter the cost, has earned them a reputation as one of the most customer-centric companies in the world.

Case Study 2: Ritz-Carlton – The Gold Standard of Customer Experience

The Ritz-Carlton is synonymous with luxury and world-class customer service. Their approach to customer service is guided by the company's motto: "We are Ladies and Gentlemen serving Ladies and Gentlemen." This reflects the respect and attention to detail that Ritz-Carlton employees bring to every customer interaction. What makes their service stand out is the level of personalization and anticipation of customer needs.

Key Takeaways:

- **Empowering Employees**: Every Ritz-Carlton employee, from the front desk to housekeeping, is empowered to spend up to $2,000 per guest, per incident, to resolve customer complaints or create memorable experiences. This autonomy allows employees to solve problems on the spot, enhancing customer satisfaction.

- **Personalization**: Ritz-Carlton excels at personalizing the guest experience. Employees are trained to take note of guests' preferences, whether it's their favorite drink or the way they like their room set up. These details are recorded and used to tailor future interactions, ensuring that every guest feels like a VIP.

- **Anticipating Needs**: Rather than waiting for guests to ask for something, Ritz-Carlton employees are trained to anticipate their needs. Whether it's offering an umbrella before a guest steps out into the rain or leaving a handwritten note in a guest's room, these small acts of thoughtfulness leave a lasting impression.

Chapter 10: Case Studies and Real-World Examples

Lesson: Empowering employees to make decisions and personalize the customer experience builds strong relationships. The Ritz-Carlton shows that when employees are trusted and given the right tools, they can create memorable experiences that go beyond customer expectations.

Case Study 3: Apple – The Power of Simplicity and Support

Apple has built its reputation on innovative products, but its customer service is also a key part of its success. Apple's commitment to providing excellent support through its Genius Bars, customer-friendly policies, and well-trained staff has set a high standard for tech companies.

Key Takeaways:

- **In-Store Support**: Apple's Genius Bars offer face-to-face support for customers who need help with their devices. This in-person service provides a high level of convenience and allows customers to get quick, expert help when they encounter issues.

- **Simplifying the Customer Journey**: Apple's product setup and customer support processes are designed to be as simple as possible. Whether it's unboxing a new iPhone or navigating the repair process, Apple makes it easy for customers to get started, get support, and stay engaged with their products.

- **Customer Education**: Apple invests in customer education, offering workshops, tutorials, and one-on-one training sessions at their stores. These resources help customers get the most out of their products, enhancing satisfaction and reducing the need for support in the future.

Lesson: Simplifying the customer experience and offering accessible, expert support can turn potentially frustrating situations into positive ones. Apple demonstrates that combining convenience with well-trained support staff can drive both customer satisfaction and loyalty.

Case Study 4: Southwest Airlines – Putting People First

Southwest Airlines has built its brand on the idea that happy employees lead to happy customers. Their customer service philosophy focuses on friendliness, low fares, and the belief that flying should be a pleasant experience. By fostering a company culture that prioritizes both employees and customers, Southwest has become one of the most beloved airlines in the U.S.

Key Takeaways:

- **Customer-Centric Culture**: Southwest's leadership believes that if they treat their employees well, those employees will, in turn, treat customers well. This philosophy has created a company culture where employees are encouraged to be friendly, personable, and go the extra mile for passengers.

- **Flexibility and Understanding**: Southwest is known for its flexible policies, such as no change fees and two free checked bags. These customer-friendly policies reduce friction and make the travel experience more enjoyable, leading to greater customer loyalty.

- **Employee Engagement**: Southwest empowers its employees to be themselves and engage with customers in a genuine way. This creates an atmosphere of warmth and friendliness, which customers appreciate—especially in an industry often associated with stress.

Lesson: A customer-first culture begins with how you treat your employees. When employees feel valued and empowered, they are more likely to deliver exceptional service to customers. Southwest's success shows that focusing on people—both employees and customers—leads to long-term loyalty and brand strength.

Applying These Lessons to Your Own Business

While the businesses highlighted in these case studies may differ in size and industry, the lessons they provide are universal. Here's how you can apply these principles to your own **Service First** business:

1. **Empower Your Team**: Empower your employees to make decisions and resolve issues on the spot. When employees feel trusted, they're more likely to go the extra mile to provide great service.

2. **Personalize the Experience**: Look for opportunities to personalize interactions with customers. Even small details, like using a customer's name or remembering their preferences, can have a big impact on loyalty.

3. **Focus on Employee Happiness**: Happy employees lead to happy customers. By fostering a positive, supportive workplace culture, you'll create a team that's motivated to deliver outstanding service.

4. **Be Proactive**: Don't wait for customers to come to you with problems — anticipate their needs and resolve issues before they arise. Whether it's offering a helpful tip or addressing a potential issue, proactive service makes customers feel valued.

5. **Simplify the Process**: Make it easy for customers to do business with you. Whether it's simplifying product setup, offering clear instructions, or providing accessible support, streamlining the customer experience leads to higher satisfaction.

Conclusion

As we've seen in these case studies, exceptional customer service is not just about resolving issues — it's about creating meaningful, memorable experiences that keep customers coming back. Whether you're running a small business or a global brand, the principles of **Service First** apply across the board: empower your team, personalize interactions, anticipate needs, and prioritize the happiness of both your employees and customers.

By adopting these lessons and continuously striving to improve, you can build a business that stands out for its commitment to service. Great customer service is an investment in your brand's future, and when done right, it leads to long-lasting success.

Chapter 10: Case Studies and Real-World Examples

Appendix A: Customer Service Checklists

The following checklists are designed to help you and your team ensure that you're delivering exceptional customer service across all interactions. Use these as a guide to regularly evaluate and improve your service delivery.

Customer Interaction Checklist

- Use this checklist to review individual customer interactions, whether they occur via phone, email, live chat, or in-person.
- Did I greet the customer warmly and professionally?
- Did I address the customer by name, where appropriate?
- Was my tone empathetic and appropriate to the situation?
- Did I actively listen to the customer's concerns without interrupting?
- Did I provide clear, concise, and accurate information?
- Was the solution provided in a timely manner?
- Did I offer the customer additional assistance or follow-up?
- Was I polite and professional throughout the interaction?
- Did I thank the customer for their business and feedback?
- Did I log the interaction accurately and follow company protocols?

Written Communication Checklist

This checklist helps ensure written communications, such as emails, tickets, or letters, meet customer service standards.

Appendix A: Customer Service Checklists

- Did I use the customer's name and personalize the message?
- Is my tone professional, yet friendly and approachable?
- Did I avoid jargon and write in a way that the customer can easily understand?
- Was the response clear and did it address the customer's concern directly?
- Did I proofread the message for spelling and grammar errors?
- Did I include all necessary information (order numbers, details, etc.)?
- Did I offer a clear next step or solution for the customer?
- Did I respond within the appropriate time frame?
- Did I close the email with a polite, professional, and helpful tone?
- Did I use templates appropriately, ensuring the message doesn't feel automated or impersonal?

Complaint Resolution Checklist

Use this checklist to ensure complaints are handled professionally and with a focus on resolution, leaving the customer feeling valued.

- Did I acknowledge the customer's issue promptly?
- Did I express empathy and apologize for the inconvenience?
- Was I calm and professional, regardless of the customer's attitude?
- Did I listen actively to the customer's full concern before responding?
- Did I offer a clear and appropriate solution to resolve the issue?
- Was I honest and transparent in my communication?

- Did I provide a timeline for when the issue will be resolved?
- Did I follow up with the customer after the resolution?
- Did I thank the customer for bringing the issue to my attention?
- Was the issue documented accurately for future reference?

Appendix A: Customer Service Checklists

Appendix B: Tools and Resources for Managing Customer Relationships

Here are some essential tools and resources that can help you manage customer relationships and deliver **Service First** experiences:

1. Customer Relationship Management (CRM) Software

CRM software helps you track interactions, manage customer data, and personalize your communication. Some popular CRM tools include:

- **Salesforce**: A comprehensive CRM platform that offers tools for sales, customer service, and marketing automation.

- **HubSpot CRM**: A free, user-friendly CRM tool that integrates with email, sales, and marketing automation tools.

- **Zoho CRM**: An affordable CRM option with customization features for small and growing businesses.

- **Zendesk**: A CRM designed specifically for customer support and ticketing, with features for tracking support requests and communication history.

2. Customer Feedback Tools

Collecting and analyzing feedback is essential for continuous improvement. Here are some tools to help you gather customer opinions:

- **SurveyMonkey**: An easy-to-use tool for creating and distributing customer satisfaction surveys.

- **Google Forms**: A free, simple option for creating feedback forms and collecting responses.

- **Typeform**: A more interactive and customizable survey tool that can help increase response rates.

- **Qualtrics**: A robust feedback platform designed for businesses looking to gather deep customer insights and analytics.

3. Help Desk and Ticketing Systems

Help desk systems allow you to track, prioritize, and respond to customer service requests efficiently:

- **Zendesk Support**: A powerful help desk and ticketing system designed to manage customer support across multiple channels.

- **Freshdesk**: A cloud-based help desk software that offers a variety of tools for managing customer inquiries and improving team productivity.

- **Helpscout**: A simple and customer-friendly help desk system that focuses on creating personal customer interactions.

- **Jira Service Desk**: A help desk solution designed for technical support teams, particularly those offering IT and software-related services.

4. Self-Service Platforms

Building a self-service platform helps customers find answers on their own, reducing the pressure on your support team:

- **Zendesk Guide**: An easy-to-use platform for creating a customer knowledge base, tutorials, and FAQs.

- **Helpjuice**: A tool that helps businesses create detailed knowledge bases for customer self-service.

- **Document360**: A platform for creating an online knowledge base and support documentation that customers can access anytime.

- **Confluence**: A collaborative platform where teams can create and share knowledge bases internally and externally.

Appendix B: Tools and Resources for Managing Customer Relationships

Appendix C: Training Exercises for Customer Service Teams

Use these exercises to train your team and improve customer service skills.

1. Role-Playing Scenarios

Set up role-playing exercises that simulate common customer service interactions to help your team practice:

- **Handling a Complaint**: One person plays the customer, presenting a complaint, while the other plays the support agent. Focus on listening, empathy, and problem-solving skills.

- **Upset Customer**: Practice defusing an emotionally charged situation. Train your team to remain calm, acknowledge the customer's emotions, and provide a solution.

- **Difficult Request**: Have one team member act as a customer with an unusual or difficult request. The goal is to balance company policy with creative problem-solving.

2. Active Listening Drill

This exercise improves active listening skills, which are crucial for understanding customer needs:

Appendix C: Training Exercises for Customer Service Teams

- **Exercise**: Pair employees up and have one person share a story about a recent experience. The listener must repeat back what they heard without interpretation or judgment, ensuring they fully understand before responding.

3. Speed Challenges

Challenge your team to respond quickly and efficiently to customer inquiries while maintaining high service standards:

- **Exercise**: Present employees with a series of rapid-fire customer inquiries and see how quickly they can resolve each one. Focus on balancing speed with quality and accuracy.

4. Problem-Solving Brainstorm

Encourage creative thinking and collaboration by presenting a challenging customer service scenario and having your team brainstorm solutions together:

- **Exercise**: Give your team a hypothetical problem (e.g., a major product defect or service delay). Have them work together to come up with a plan for addressing the issue, communicating with customers, and preventing future problems.

Appendix D: Customer Service Scripts and Templates

Here are a few scripts and templates to help your team provide consistent and high-quality service:

1. First Response Template (Email)

Subject: We've Received Your Request – We're Here to Help!

Hi [Customer Name],

Thank you for reaching out to us. We've received your request and will work to resolve your issue as quickly as possible. Our support team will be in touch with you within [response time] to provide assistance.

In the meantime, if you have any additional details to share, please feel free to reply to this email.

Thank you for your patience!

Best regards,
[Your Name]
[Company Name] Support Team

2. Follow-Up After Resolution (Email)

Subject: How Was Your Experience?

Hi [Customer Name],

I hope your issue has been resolved to your satisfaction. We'd love to hear about your experience and make sure everything went smoothly.

If you have any feedback, feel free to reply to this email or complete this short survey [link]. We're always looking for ways to improve and ensure our customers are happy.

Thank you for being a valued customer, and don't hesitate to reach out if you need anything else!

Best regards,
[Your Name]
[Company Name] Support Team

3. De-Escalation Script (Phone)

"I understand how frustrating this must be for you, and I want to make sure we get this resolved as quickly as possible. Let me walk you through the next steps and what we can do to fix this."

Appendix E: Crisis Management in Customer Service

How to Handle Major Service Failures

Every business will face a crisis at some point, whether it's a product recall, a significant service outage, or a public relations issue. Being prepared to manage these situations with a **Service First** approach can help maintain customer trust, even in the most challenging times.

Steps for Effective Crisis Management:

- **Acknowledge the Issue Quickly**: As soon as a problem arises, acknowledge it publicly to your customers. Transparency is key in maintaining trust.

- **Communicate Regularly**: Keep your customers updated throughout the crisis, even if you don't have all the answers yet. Silence creates uncertainty, and uncertainty breeds frustration.

- **Apologize Sincerely**: Always offer a heartfelt apology when things go wrong. Customers are generally forgiving when they feel the business is accountable.

- **Offer a Solution**: Whether it's a refund, a free replacement, or extra support, make sure you're offering a solution that addresses the issue head-on.

- **Learn and Improve**: After the crisis is over, conduct a thorough review of what went wrong, how it was handled, and how you can prevent it in the future.

Appendix E: Crisis Management in Customer Service

Appendix F: Building Customer Service into Your Company's Mission and Brand

Aligning Customer Service with Your Brand Values

Customer service should be an extension of your brand. This section could guide business owners on how to integrate customer service into their company's mission and values, ensuring that every customer interaction reinforces their brand identity.

Key Questions for Business Owners:

- What do we want our customers to feel after every interaction with us?

- How can our customer service reflect our core values (e.g., innovation, transparency, community)?

- What tone and style should we use in customer communications?

- What do we want customers to remember about our brand after each interaction?

Appendix F: Building Customer Service into Your Company's Mission and Brand

Appendix G: The Role of Customer Service in Building Business Resilience

Creating a Customer Service Plan for Uncertain Times

The recent global events, like the COVID-19 pandemic, have shown how important it is for businesses to be adaptable. This section could focus on how strong customer service builds resilience, helping businesses weather crises, economic downturns, and sudden changes.

Resilient Customer Service Strategies:

- **Adaptability**: Train your team to handle rapid changes, such as shifts to remote customer support or increased demand during crises.

- **Communication**: During times of uncertainty, customers need reassurance. Regular, clear communication goes a long way in building trust during unpredictable events.

- **Flexibility**: Be prepared to offer flexible policies (e.g., extended return periods, delayed payment options) to help your customers during challenging times.

Appendix G: The Role of Customer Service in Building Business Resilience

Appendix H: Customer Retention vs. Customer Acquisition

Why Retention is More Important
Acquiring new customers is far more expensive than retaining existing ones. Adding a section that delves into the value of focusing on customer retention and loyalty would provide extra insight for business owners.

Key Stats:

- **It costs 5-7 times more to acquire a new customer than to retain an existing one.**
- **Increasing customer retention by just 5% can boost profits by 25% to 95%.**

Retention Strategies:

- **Loyalty Programs**: Rewarding repeat customers encourages them to stay engaged.
- **Personalized Offers**: Use customer data to offer tailored promotions based on past purchases.
- **Exclusive Access**: Provide your most loyal customers with early access to new products or services, reinforcing their value to your business.

Appendix H: Customer Retention vs. Customer Acquisition

Appendix I: The Future of Customer Service

Trends and Innovations Shaping Customer Service
It might be helpful to conclude the book by discussing future trends in customer service, such as AI, automation, and the increasing role of data analytics. This section could help business owners prepare for emerging customer service technologies.

Key Trends:

- **AI-Powered Personalization**: AI tools that can predict customer needs and offer tailored solutions in real time.

- **Automation with a Human Touch**: Striking a balance between automated self-service and human interaction will become even more crucial.

- **Customer Service as a Revenue Driver**: Customer service is increasingly becoming a key differentiator and driver of business growth, not just a cost center.

Appendix I: The Future of Customer Service

Appendix J: The Psychology of Great Customer Service

Understanding Customer Psychology
A brief section on how understanding customer psychology can enhance service quality. Business owners could learn about emotional triggers that impact customer satisfaction, how to build positive emotional connections, and why certain interactions leave a lasting impression.

Emotional Drivers to Leverage:

- **Trust**: Customers need to trust your brand before they feel loyal.

- **Belonging**: Creating a sense of community or belonging can encourage customers to engage more deeply.

- **Anticipation**: Surprising and delighting customers by anticipating their needs can create lasting positive experiences.

www.ingramcontent.com/pod-product-compliance
Lightning Source LLC
Chambersburg PA
CBHW052153220526
45471CB00004B/1653